D1756725

30150   019978854

Of Relations and the Dead

EXPLORATIONS IN ANTHROPOLOGY
A University College London Series

Series Editors: Barbara Bender, John Gledhill and Bruce Kapferer

Joan Bestard-Camps, *What's in a Relative? Household and Family in Formentera*

Henk Driessen, *On the Spanish-Moroccan Frontier: A Study in Ritual, Power and Ethnicity*

Alfred Gell, *The Anthropology of Time: Cultural Construction of Temporal Maps and Images*

Time Ingold, David Riches and James Woodburn (eds), *Hunters and Gatherers*

   Volume 1. *History, Evolution and Social Change*
   Volume 2. *Property, Power and Ideology*

Bruce Kapferer, *A Celebration of Demons* (2nd edn.)

Guy Lanoue, *Brothers: The Politics of Violence among the Sekani of Northern British Columbia*

Jadran Mimica, *Intimations of Infinity: The Mythopoeia of the Iqwaye Counting System and Number*

Barry Morris, *Domesticating Resistance: The Dhan-Gadi Aborigines and the Australian State*

Thomas C. Paterson, *The Inca Empire: The Formation and Disintegration of a Pre-Capitalist State*

Max and Eleanor Rimoldi, *Hahalis and the Labour of Love: A Social Movement on Buka Island*

Pnina Werbner, *The Migration Process: Capital, Gifts and Offerings among Pakistanis in Britain*

Joel S. Kahn, *Constituting the Minangkabu: Peasants, Culture, and Modernity in Colonial Indonesia*

Gisli Pálsson, *Beyond Boundaries: Understanding, Translation and Anthropological Discourse*

Stephen Nugent, *Amazonian Caboclo Society*

Barbara Bender, *Landscape: Politics and Perspectives*

Christopher Tilley (ed.), *Interpretative Archaeology*

Ernest S. Burch, Jr. and Linda J. Ellanna, *Key Issues in Hunter-Gatherer Research*

Daniel Miller, *Modernity – An Ethnographic Approach: Dualism and Mass Consumption in Trinidad*

Robert Pool, *Dialogue and the Interpretation of Illness: Conversations in a Cameroon Village*

Of Relations and the Dead

Four Societies Viewed from the Angle of Their Exchanges

Cécile Barraud, Daniel de Coppet, André Iteanu and Raymond Jamous

Translated by
Stephen J. Suffern

BERG
Oxford/Providence, USA

English edition
first published in 1994 by
Berg Publishers
Editorial offices:
150 Cowley Road, Oxford, OX4 1JJ, UK
221 Waterman Road, Providence, RI 02906, USA

French edition: Des relations et des morts; étude de quatre
sociétés vues sous l'angle des échanges, in: Différences, valeurs,
hiérarchie; textes offerts à Louis Dumont, Jean-Claude Galey
(ed), 1984, EHESS-Paris.

Library of Congress Cataloging-in-Publication Data
A catalogue record for this book is available from the British
Library.

British Library Cataloguing in Publication Data
A catalogue record for this book is available from the British
Library.

ISBN 0 85496 953 5 (Cloth)
     1 85973 046 9

Printed and bound in Great Britain by WBC, Bridgend, Mid Glan

'Time you altogether dead-finish, Nirawa, where you stop?'
'Me no savvy, master. Missie (missionary) he speak body belong
me go in ground, wind belong me go up-tree (on high, aloft, etc.).
Me think he speak altogether gammon too much. Me think time
me fellow dead-finish me stop altogether same pig.'

from Asterisk
Isles of illusion[1]
Letters from the South Seas

1. *Isles of illusion. Letters from the South Seas* by Asterisk (pen name of Robert James Fletcher). First published by Constable & Co. Ltd, London, in 1923. Present edition by Bohun Lynch, Century, London,1986, p.38. Marie-Joëlle Dardelin called our attention to this text. The Melanesian speaker is addressing a Protestant minister.

Contents

Introduction

This article grew out of the confluence of a number of different factors. The first was an epistemological problem, the others were more fortuitous, though they stemmed from the encounter over a period of years of a group of scholars who have patiently pooled their data on various societies, their analytical efforts and their theoretical insights.[2] It is an exacting task we have set ourselves, but bolder still perhaps is our effort here to render homage, however inadequate, to Professor Louis Dumont – to the man, to his work and to his practice of social anthropology in the service of comparative sociology. It is our hope that in this book, our joint endeavour published over our common signature, the homage we intend is clear.

Anthropology, availing itself of the wealth of data collected by Thurnwald and Malinowski on the Melanesian Islands and enriched by the publication in 1923–4 of Marcel Mauss' *Essai sur le Don*, has since striven to find an explanation for the prestations and counter-prestations which punctuate the life of the societies of the region. These exchanges have, it is true, the advantage of being easily observable and, some believe, even quantifiable. However, what was certainly most reassuring was that simple observation seemed to reveal the transfer of objects among individuals who could be considered the actors of the exchanges. It thus seemed possible to fall back comfortably on different variants of models dependent on economic considerations, or on systems already identified in the history of European societies. Certain observers sought to unearth in traditional societies a fascinating egalitarian primitive communism. Others saw in these societies' exchanges an equivalent to violent confrontations, and analysed them as ways to consolidate or contest the pre-eminence of certain individuals. The debate continues today, at least between theorists of profit and their adversaries who stress conspicuous spending and conspicuous waste.

2. With regard to the Introduction of the french version, the authors would like to thank Dominique Casajus for his suggestions and criticism and Haude Le Guen for her attentive reading.

1

Structuralism, which considers all societies' exchanges as constituting just so many systems of 'exchange,' has sought to establish the general, even universal, reach of its proposition. The exchange of women offered a considerable body of data whose variations lent themselves to a rigorous ordering. The analysis of marriage-alliance revealed more powerful rules than those which had previously emerged from the study of descent and inheritance, both of which had long intrigued adherents of corporate group analysis. The principal advances in this field were van Wouden's discovery of 'asymmetric connubium' and Claude Lévi-Strauss' systematic treatment of marriage-alliance. By laying bare 'the elementary structures of kinship', the latter was able to contrast different systems all founded on a universal logic of exchange, and to formulate distinctions among various sorts of restricted or generalised reciprocity.

The imposition of a distinction between nature and culture thus led to the same consequences as economically oriented explanatory efforts. The subjects of exchanges remained sharply distinguished from their objects, with however a notable shift in the meaning of the terms. In the case of marriages and marriage systems, the subjects were certainly still 'men', but this time in the narrow sense, since the objects of exchange had become none other than women. This intrusion in structuralism of a power relationship, although the theory has generally taken pains not to venture onto that ground, is surprising, and all the more so since men's power over exchanges of women seems to be a postulate arrived at a priori, of a logical nature, whose acceptance, in any event, implicitly concedes that women cannot be denied their quality as a value (Lévi-Strauss 1967: 60). Our observations are not, of course, intended as a protest to defend the feminine gender against its opposite. We simply wish to call attention to two points: the violence done here to the absolute distinction between subject and object; and the explicit recourse had to a consideration of values. The 'exchange of women', in other words, refuses obligingly to don its theoretical straitjacket.

In structuralist theory, furthermore, the 'exchange of women' is sundered from a society's overall system of exchanges, dealt with in isolation, and made, beyond the bounds of a given society, the sole object of comparison with other societies. It thus assumes the character of a universal social phenomenon within the more general formula of 'reciprocity as the norm'. The segregation from all others of this particular exchange, then used as the basis for propositions deemed universal, glosses over the necessary study of each society's entire system of exchanges. It prejudges the relative weights which are assumed, here and there, by goods, women and men taken in marriage or adopted, the dead who perish violently and those who die naturally, and even the constituent elements which, for a particular society, make up and circulate in the universe it constructs for itself.

Our perspective is more modest, in the sense that it does not lead us to formulate universals directly, on the basis of a comparison of social traits selected in advance for their significance. We thus attempt to avoid extracting from the whole of a given society certain phenomena which, it seems more than likely, can only be understood in relation to that whole, and strive to understand the ensemble of each society's exchanges as a system which may be compared to other such systems which analysis brings to light in other societies. The comparison attempted here is thus not restricted to exchanges of women, but deals with the entire systems of exchanges of several societies considered as wholes.

This approach encountered numerous difficulties, of which the most perplexing was certainly the famous distinction between subjects and objects. Can it be said that the societies studied here do not recognise the same distinction as ours? If they do not, how can we grasp the logic of their organisation of the relations between persons and things, given the subjection of our own thought to the subject–object distinction? How can we understand their exchanges when the substantialist approach most commonly adopted, attentive only to the passage of objects between subjects, turns its back on the very relational logic which we seek to lay bare? Linear causality and the principles of non-contradiction and the excluded middle are adequate for a logic of substances. But is there not something more to a relation than objects being transferred between subjects? It is at this point that we are obliged to return to Mauss, despite the suggestion that on these questions he fell prey to a sort of hoax, adopting his indigenous informants' theories as his own.[3] If Mauss enjoys so much success today among those who are attempting to propose an interpretation of exchanges, it is because by doing violence to the frontier between subjects and objects he reflects a profound reality of numerous exchange systems

---

3. Lévi-Strauss raises this objection in his introduction to the collection of Mauss' works published under the title *Sociologie et anthropologie*, Paris, Presses Universitaires de France, 1950, p. XXXVIII.

– that the objects convey something of the persons who set them in motion. For Mauss, exchanges cease to be inexplicable 'if we realise that there exists, above all, an intertwining of spiritual ties between things which are to some degree soul, and individuals and groups that treat each other to some degree as things' (Mauss 1924 (1950: 163); our translation). Even our own civilisation, from its very beginnings, has constantly shifted the frontier separating subject and object. Raymond Williams has dedicated a long article to tracing these fluctuations, slippages and inversions of meaning from the Middle Ages to the present. The concept of the subject has indeed taken on multiple and somewhat contradictory senses in the course of history, signifying initially a person subject to a sovereign or the substance of things, before becoming the thinking *subject* 'from the operations of which the independent existence of all other things must be deduced as *objects* thrown before this consciousness'. (Williams 1976: 261). One could not better express the remarkable declaration of independence of the subject, raised in the guise of the individual to the rank of absolute value. It is surprising that anthropology, in its efforts to understand nonmodern societies, has not given more attention to its own difficulties in wielding the notions of subject and object. It has doubtless been blind, or at least too complacent, in imposing as universals distinctions subject, one might say, to different histories even in the various European cultures. This approach has entitled us to numerous dissertations on animism, the prelogical mind and similar matters.

The questioning of the separation of subject and object which constitutes Mauss' principal theme in his essay *The Gift* (cf. D. Casajus 1984: 65–78) goes hand-in-hand in the materials he analyses with the non-separation of the economic, jural, social and religious spheres. He is led finally to suggest that exchanges are 'total social phenomena'. We would have advanced no further were it not for the work of Polanyi, for whom 'the outstanding discovery of recent historical and anthropological research is that man's economy, as a rule, is submerged in his social relationships' (Polanyi 1957: 46), and for that of Louis Dumont, who judges it characteristic of the ideology of 'modern' societies to consider the individual as a whole and an absolute value, in contrast with all 'non-modern' societies, in which the individual subjects are entirely subordinated to the social whole which alone is bearer of value.

If we admit that, in societies in which the individual, the 'empirical agent', is not 'regarded as the indivisible, "elementary" man, both a biological being and a thinking subject' (Dumont 1980: 9), the subject must be understood as part of an order in which he participates at his appropriate place, and that the relation between subject and object is consequently subordinated to something else situated outside of this relation itself, we are led to recognise explicitly that, in these societies, a hierarchy of values governs the relation between subject and object. If in Western societies, on the contrary, we seem to be able to do without such a hierarchy, it is because the individual-subject considers himself – with the immense consequences of which we are well aware – the supreme value, separated from the object, which has become the entire universe that the individual expects to rule.

Were we to try to characterise schematically the difference between modern and non-modern societies in the light of the distinction between subject and object, it might be said that the former have progressively narrowed the category 'subject' to individuals alone, while confining Nature in that of 'object'. In the course of this evolution, individual subjects have become the absolute value, while objects have lost all access to transcendence. In contrast, though non-modern societies also recognise a distinction between subject and object, this distinction is not absolute and does not enter into the definition of the nature of an entity, so much so that what in one circumstance is 'object' in another may equally well be 'subject'. The attribution of the quality of subject or object is subordinated to an encompassing system, a whole, which determines assignment to the appropriate category. A recognition of the fluctuating character of the subject–object distinction in these societies requires us to question the absolute character it has assumed in ours.

Before undertaking our comparative study of exchanges in four non-modern societies, we should not only stress the need to avoid drawing too rigid a distinction between subject and object, but should also define more precisely what we mean by exchanges, at least at this preliminary stage. We suggest that exchanges are *all activities in the course of which something is seen to circulate*. We stress here observable circulation, taking care not to reduce this circulation simply to exchanges between partners, that is, not to adopt straightway an individual reference point, be it that of a physical person or that of a circumscribed group. In accordance with this view, the word 'exchanges' does not necessarily imply reciprocity for us, any more than it excludes a gratuitous gift. Polemics about the nature of circulation have not led to satisfactory conclusions, and to avoid the premature incursion of definitional questions, we have chosen to start from the conceptions in use in the societies themselves with regard to their exchanges, broadening our understanding of exchanges thereafter through a comparative approach. We have a twofold objective: to evaluate the relative weight of exchanges in the structure of each society, and to develop new criteria for the comparison of non-modern societies among themselves.

The four societies studied are the Orokaiva of Papua New Guinea, the 'Are'are of the Solomon Islands, Tanebar-Evav in Eastern Indonesia, and the Iqar'iyen of the Moroccan Rif.[4] We first examine the vocabulary used in relation to exchanges in each society and offer a preliminary comparison of this data. Thereafter, the exchanges of each of the four are analysed in the 'movement of the whole' of the society, to use Mauss' expression (Mauss 1950: 275; our translation).

---

4. For more detailed descriptions of each of these societies, the reader should consult the relevant texts cited in the bibliography.

Chapter 1

The Vocabulary of Exchanges

Orokaiva

Among the **Orokaiva**, the terms used in speaking of exchanges do not always describe them with the same degree of generality. Thus, the prestations which open the initiation, marriage and funeral rituals have no generic name, although analysis demonstrates that they form a well-defined class. By the variety of terms employed, the Orokaiva differentiate the prestations offered on each of these occasions, stressing in this case the specificity of the several rituals.

All other Orokaiva exchanges are, however, attributed by them to one of two broad categories designated by the contrasting terms *pondo* and *hande*. As a first approximation, we may say that *pondo* and its synonym *jopa* are the words used to refer to the society's most formalised exchanges, often accompanied by sumptuous rituals. *Hande*, in contrast, is the term applied to more discreet, smaller exchanges between individual subjects. However, as the disconcerted observer quickly discovers, certain exchanges of very similar appearance are sometimes called *pondo* and, in other circumstances, *hande*. For the Orokaiva do not classify their exchanges on the basis of their material aspect, but rather in accordance with the position they occupy in the society's hierarchy of values. *Hande* and *pondo* are in fact what we will designate different 'levels of exchange', corresponding to different levels of value.

This disparity in value is made manifest by the presence at all *pondo* exchanges of *amita be*, the 'true thing' or the 'true reason,'[5] which is never found at *hande* exchanges. The term *amita be* designates simultaneously the reason underlying the *pondo*, explicitly announced by the person who gives it, and the material prestation he offers, which is always principally composed of pork. The reason invoked is necessarily related to the 'social person' *hamo* – one of the aspects of the complete Orokaiva person – either of the giver

---

5. Although *amita be* has both these meanings, in the remainder of this article we will translate it simply as 'true reason'.

of the *pondo* himself or of another in whose name he offers the prestation. The giver declaims, for example: 'I give this *pondo* for the man who healed my *hamo* which was sick', or 'I give this *pondo* for the man who made my son's *hamo* grow during his initiation.' The prestation is also said to be given 'for the *hamo*' of the donee who eats the pork and thereby incorporates the 'true reason' previously announced by the giver. At a *pondo*, the giver's social person is thus linked to his donee's through the *amita be*. A 'true reason' must indeed tie the donor to every person present at a *pondo*. Thus, invited guests and even unexpected visitors are menaced with a spear by the giver when they arrive. This threat of violence to their *hamo* provides him with a 'true reason' to offer them a part of the pork distributed.

In *hande* exchanges, on the contrary, a person's *hamo* is no longer involved. What is important is his 'inside' *jo* – a second aspect of the Orokaiva person, the place where certain hidden forces are located. A *hande* prestation is given 'because of the donor's *jo*' and 'for the donee's *jo*'. Such offerings are less formalised than those of a *pondo*, are given more discreetly, often in closed baskets whose contents are thus concealed from view, and no 'true reason' is invoked.

In explaining how a *pondo* originates, the Orokaiva always also mention the intervention of secret underlying motivations located in the giver's *jo*. When these hidden forces give rise to actions which affect the *hamo*, however, a *pondo*, which attributes social meaning to past actions, becomes obligatory. This would be the case for example when the 'sympathy', arising in his *jo*, that a person feels for a family in mourning leads him to offer them the food they need to avoid starvation. All *pondo* thus begin in the same way as *hande*, but *hande*, which involve exclusively or almost exclusively the *jo*, never attain the *pondo* level and do not contribute to the constitution of social reality. Present *pondo* give a definitive social meaning to *jo*-inspired past events, although past events do not permit predictions concerning future exchanges.

Pondo are also sharply distinguished from *hande* in another regard. Only the former always call for a return prestation, called *mine*, which must moreover be rigorously identical to what was initially given. The term *mine* designates not only a return *pondo* but more generally any 'perfect' giving in return: three areca nuts for three areca nuts, a pig for a pig of the same size, a blow for a similar blow, a man's sister given in marriage to his wife's brother, help of the same kind given for help received. Every *pondo* explicitly proposes a 'true reason' which was previously only potential but which will only be recognised as completely definitive once the *pondo* is returned, that is, after its identical *pondo mine*. The hidden forces originating in the first feast-giver's *jo* are thus subordinated to the exchange system, since in the end a superior, social meaning has been attributed to an event, which can then be filed away and forgotten.

A resourceful man is one who knows how to use *mine* to his advantage, to keep a matter open when he wishes or, on the contrary, to extricate himself from it by closing it rapidly. The time of Orokaiva society is constructed of, and its rhythm established by, the periods between *pondo* and their return *mine*. Variations in the length of these intervals are one measure of the part left in exchanges to human initiative. In the broadest context, even the initiation ritual may be understood as opening an interval of life between two prestations. At the initiation of a generation of children, the spirits offer pigs to men, and they receive a sort of *mine* at the same children's funerals, when the latters' corpses return one by one to the bush in the form of wild animals (Iteanu 1983a).

The other Orokaiva exchanges which have no generic name and are each designated by a specific term must also be incorporated in a comprehensive analysis of the society's exchange system. As we shall see below, these exchanges form a third category associated with yet another aspect of the person, distinct from both *hamo* and *jo*.

'Are'are

The **'Are'are** have no word equivalent to our term 'exchange'. When speaking of what we would call exchanges, they have recourse to three notions to designate certain stages in their unfolding: 'return', 'linked succession', and 'stop'.

'Return', *rikiriki* or *oorisi*, is the most usual manner of referring to an exchange, and in fact all exchanges may be considered 'returns', without its being necessary to specify in each case the reason for so characterising them. A 'return' is an elementary unit, a kind of indivisible fact. It is the smallest conceivable sequence of the immense ensemble constituted by all the society's exchanges, whose complete cycle is never fully plotted out. 'Return' is also the most neutral way of speaking of an exchange, since it incorporates secondarily two more specific ideas, replacement by something identical and replacement by something equivalent. Since 'return' embraces both these meanings, it refers to a phenomenon broader than reciprocity. We must indeed be very careful not to confuse 'return' with the act of 'giving back', as our Western way of thinking would normally lead us to. If we substitute the idea of 'giving back' for 'return', we surreptitiously slip the subject back into a dominant position, while in this Melanesian society the subject who 'gives back' is subordinated to the 'return' itself. This can be sensed in such expressions as: 'You cannot not do that', or 'The thing cannot not "return"'. Thus 'return', a notion applicable to all exchanges in 'Are'are society, makes reference to an irresistible overall movement testifying to the existence of a superior order which prevails at the same time over both subjects and objects of exchange.

'Linked succession', *aahia*, is the principal means of articulation of the system of circulation, as well as its most dramatic moment, charged with antagonistic values. It consists in connecting an additional event to a series, but this connecting is absolutely ineluctable and expresses the immense force of an inexorable process in which each new event is, in a sense, piled on to the one which precedes it. The term 'linked succession' is used when speaking of prestations and counter-prestations in which the giver's payment of a debt owed represents the creation of a new debt for the receiver. The series compose a system to which the partners themselves are subordinated.

'Linked succession' assumes particular importance in two contexts, funeral feasts and sequential murders, where it represents the ritual fulfilment of a duty of capital importance for the deceased. When he receives the homage of his funeral feast, an 'Are'are who has died of illness – whose death is always said to be caused by his ancestors – is 'covered' by a chain of ritual acts which transforms the deceased himself into an ancestor. His relatives, and with them the entire society, carry out the 'linked succession' appropriate in the higher order of circulation. 'Linked succession' both effectuates this transformation and ratifies it.

Similarly, the last victim in a murder series must be 'covered' by a new one; a new victim's interrupted 'breath' covers and appeases the former's. Each successive murder thus settles a previous one. There is no beginning or end but rather, above all, a sort of filing away of the past without the least regard for the future. From the standpoint of the values of the partners, this 'linked succession' is, for one, in perfect conformity with the norm and has the character of a settlement (this perspective is attributed greater value by the society), while the other perceives it as 'transgressive', as 'overstepping the bounds'. Indeed, an act of vengeance is felt as proper and soothing by the person who commits it, but is experienced as a new challenge by the most recent victim's family. Not only are the subjects' opposed points of view subordinated here to a superior system which orders them, but a hierarchical relationship exists between their positions. The former is encompassing and bears witness to the superior order of the society, while the latter is socially residual.[6] We will see below that these series of 'linked successions' form part of a system of circulation of all the 'murdered' dead.

The third fundamental notion of 'Are'are exchange vocabulary is the 'stop' or 'break', *suu*, *toto* or *mou*. This punctuation point is associated with the idea of a fall (the sunset), a sinking (of a stone to the bottom), and always takes the form of a prestation of shell-money. All 'stops' are monetary, while 'linked successions' are never exclusively so. As we demonstrate below, 'stops' are not governed by the principle of equalisation of losses; rather, on the contrary, the money offered is always a supplementary prestation which intervenes at a moment when the number of victims on each side is equal. Murder series are characterised by 'stops' between particular partners who may then contract marriages. A 'stop' should be seen as a special kind of linkage signifying the closing of the preceding sequence. The power of money to close a series and re-establish peace demonstrates how superior it is in value to all things and, in particular, to men.

Our sketch of 'Are'are exchange vocabulary reveals, over and above the partners to and objects of exchanges, the presence of a higher order, a circulation, which though never specifically named is always implicit. It is this encompassing system which we analyse below. The strict system into which 'Are'are exchanges are organised necessarily implies extremely strong constraints. The

---

6. If one insists, on the contrary, on stressing the offended party's viewpoint, the act is incorrectly interpreted as a challenge turned toward the future, while here it is in fact fundamentally a 'linked succession' necessary to 'cover' a certain past. By introducing strategic calculation as the underlying reason for such an act, the observer would thus be imposing his modern prejudices, in a determination to 'discover' a calculated transgression. This viewpoint reduces exchanges to means used by and for individuals.

vocabulary which we have described would remain in a sense up in the air, without real foundation (*hora'aa* 'gratuitous', 'without supreme sanction'), if the exchanges practised by the living were not placed in the context of 'acts' accomplished by the dead, since it is the ancestors who cause sickness, death and marriages, and give their names to newborn children. The ancestors are at both ends of the chain! Further, and consequently, the three notions which are used to speak of exchanges always interpret them retrospectively. Exchanges give a definitive meaning to the past, but say nothing about the present or the future. They are, first of all and in every case, a necessary putting in order of the past. If they leave an opening toward the future, it is only as repetition. To consider these exchanges, on the contrary, as a series of drafts drawn on the future or as 'producing' some sort of protean 'becoming' would be to impose our modern manner of grasping them. The two points of view are diametrically opposed and founded on radically different ideologies.[7]

Tanebar-Evav

In contrast to the two Melanesian societies discussed where exchanges involve persons specially assembled for ceremonial purposes, at **Tanebar-Evav**[8] they occur either between 'houses', which are permanent institutional groups, between the entire society called *lór-haratut* and other societies of the same type or, finally, between the living and various categories of supernatural beings. Further, while in Melanesia only negative marriage rules are encountered, at Tanebar-Evav the positive rule of asymmetric marriage with the matrilateral cross-cousin creates a tight skein of inter-marriage ties which each person is bound to respect. Finally, the village's meticulous, immutable layout on its island, and the position of the island among the villages of the archipelago, as well as the unalterable, hereditary distribution of the most important social and ritual functions among a small group of initiates, leave only a residual place for individual initiative. These strict, unchanging dispositions reflect the extreme formalisation of relations

7. By ideology we understand 'a social set of representations; the set of ideas and values that are common in a society (= global ideology); a specified part of the global ideology : economic ideology' (L. Dumont, 1986: 279).
8. Tanebar-Evav is an island in the Kei archipelago which forms part of the South-Eastern Moluccas, in Eastern Indonesia. The sole village on the island bears the same name.

among the 'houses' as well as between the whole society and its various supernatural beings.

Contrary to the Melanesian cases, exchanges in such a society are not themselves the only visible structuring element, but rather coexist with a stable social morphology. At Tanebar-Evav no master word exists to refer to the entire system of exchanges as such. Rather, a great variety of terms and expressions is employed to characterise prestations and describe the parties' respective positions in the relationships created by exchanges. This linguistic profusion suggests the importance of exchanges in the society, but does not permit us easily to perceive a totality conforming to the model proposed by alliance theory.

Two great series of events set the rhythm of life at Tanebar-Evav: for approximately eight months each year, the ritual millet cultivation cycle, and during the remaining four months, the organisation of marriages and ceremonial feasts, the construction of houses and sailing-boats, and the preparation of long sea voyages among other activities. However, marriages are clearly the most important matter for each person and for the society as a whole. A detailed study of marriage ceremonies will thus be the fundamental element of our analysis of the place of exchanges in the social structure, which can only be understood by taking into account the society's encompassing ideology expressed in its values. A brief description of the millet ritual will also be necessary in order to grasp this society as a whole.

Since marriage exchanges are the most easily observed, a discussion of the terms used in connection with them will permit us immediately to delineate the notion of exchange at Tanebar-Evav. In this society, a woman is given against what we commonly call a 'marriage compensation'. The giving of this compensation is expressed by the term *ót velin*. At Tanebar-Evav, the word *ót* is used very generally with the meaning 'to do' or 'to make', as in the question '*Om ót haf kèhè?*' 'What are you doing?' The word *velin*, 'marriage compensation', contains the root *vel*, which often appears in words expressing an idea of 'doing in return'. This prestation is composed of a variety of precious goods, including old Portuguese and Dutch cannon, gongs imported from Western Indonesia, and different sorts of jewellery. It is said that the cannon offered 'replaces' – *hólók* – the woman's body. In short, three notions appear here: doing, doing in return, and replacement.

Ot velin cannot however properly be translated as 'to do (to

make) the marriage compensation' since the term here is used for
the act of offering. The word *ót* indeed often marks the establishing of a relationship between persons or things. A person comes
to visit for example, and one hands him the *maneran*, betel-leaves
and areca-nuts to chew. This is referred to as *ót maneran*, which
should be understood not as 'doing the *maneran*' but rather as 'offering the *maneran*'. The word *ót* is not used, furthermore, to express the idea of 'doing' specific sorts of work, where we would
have a tendency to say that someone 'does' such-and-such a task.
At Tanebar-Evav, a different, specific vocabulary is employed to
describe each particular kind of activity. *Ot* is, however, very frequently used in the case of ceremonial offerings, followed in each
instance by the name of the specific offering or by that of the person or supernatural being for whom it is intended. *Ot wadar*, for
example, means to offer food to a house's ancestors – *wadar*, *ót lenar*
to offer *lenar*, small plaited bags made of coconut palm leaves in
which rice is cooked, to certain supernatural beings; *ót sinuku* to
prepare and offer the *sinuku*, a ritual performed at funeral ceremonies to drive away evil sicknesses, and so forth. *Ot* can thus be
taken, very broadly, as meaning 'to engage in an activity', and is
most often employed to refer to specific ritual work. At Tanebar-
Evav no word exists, as in French or English, which expresses the
idea of work or working in general. The very notion of work is
bound up with the idea of relationship and of a certain form of
ritual activity. To give the marriage compensation is thus to perform the ritual work of creating a relationship.[9]

The root *vel* expresses the idea of 'doing in return', as we have
noted in the word *velin*, the return prestation or 'marriage compensation' in asymmetric marriage. It is also found in various terms
used in other exchanges. Thus *havel*, often accompanied by the
word *fiang*, signifies 'to give to return', 'to give in return' as, for
example, in the rare cases of *sivelek* marriage, where women, generally at least a generation apart, circulate in both directions, contrary to the rule of asymmetric marriage. The name of this type of
marriage, *sivelek*, itself implies the return of women in exchanges
which, it is said, 'zigzag like sweet-potato vines creeping along the
ground'. *Havel* also expresses the idea of selling, as in the verb

9. The word *enan*, 'price', 'cost', 'result', confirms the idea that exchange is work which leads
to a result. The wife is the 'result' – *enan* – of all the work accomplished in the various exchanges
of the marriage ceremonies. When in war a man is killed with a machete, the villagers speak of
nger ni enan 'the result of the machete'. The word *enan* is also used for the harvest, the fruit of the
community's collective effort, involving both the living and the dead.

fed-havel 'to sell to return', which in the past was used to describe the sale of sailing-boats or of a house's servants. The simple verb 'to sell' does not exist at Tanebar-Evav, and the expression *fed-havel* in no way implies the seeking of profit, but solely a separating oneself from something which is replaced by something else, in this case by various forms of money which will in turn assume their place in the society's exchanges.

The idea of return is also expressed by a synonym of *havel*, the word *il*. The villagers say for example *fiang il*, 'to give in return' the woman in a *sivelek* marriage. *Il* combines with a number of other verbal radicals to express specific forms of return.[10] *Ta piar il* expresses the action of offering prestations to the villagers' common ancestors and to the dead in general. *Piar* derives from the Indonesian word *piara* and means 'to bring up', 'to take care of' (a child, for example). *Ta piar il* thus means literally: 'We bring up the ancestors in return.' Since the ancestors brought us up by giving us food and teaching us the society's customs, it is our duty in return to protect them, to take care of them and to nourish them like children, although in a different way, by offering them prestations of food, tobacco, betel-leaves, and areca-nuts. There is here a continuous exchange or, more precisely, a constantly repeated returning to the ancestors of what each generation has received from the preceding one.

While the 'work of return' *ót velin* implies an idea of repeated movement, another of the fundamental aspects of exchange is often described as 'replacement', *hólók* or *lalin*. To 'replace' is, here, to put something in the place of a 'body', *itumun*, which may be a human body but may also, for example, be a pig, a tree trunk, or the hull of a sailing-boat. In the case of asymmetric marriage, a woman is 'replaced' by a cannon, which is one sort of money, just as a villager or a noble's servant who has been killed is 'replaced' by various kinds of money, or as an adopted male child 'replaces' his adoptive father. (Such an adoption is itself styled *ndók hólók* 'to be–to replace'.) Replacement by money generally implies the subordination of one of the parties to an exchange to the other, of the takers to the givers of a woman or an adopted child in the cases of marriage or adoption, or to the spirit Hukum, who represents the society, when murder or incest is involved. It stresses one element

10. *Ba il* 'to go–to return' or 'to come back'; *var il* 'to carry away–to return' or 'to bring something back'; *her il* 'to ask for–to return' or 'to bring someone back'; *tovuk il* 'to replace–to return' or 'to replace in exchange for'.

of a single sequence in a series of exchanges, while the idea of return suggests their general movement.

The ideas of replacement and return are both present as well when, in a *sivelek* marriage, the parties to the exchange use the expression *ta slalin*. *Slalin* is the reciprocal pronominal form of the verb *lalin* and is used in instances where reciprocal prestations of the same nature are offered, a canoe for a canoe, a woman for a woman. It is probably best translated: 'We replace mutually'. In this case, the replacement is not accomplished through the intermediary of money.

Finally, it is notable that in the expression *ót velin*, 'the ritual work of return' in marriage, only the giving in return is emphasised and not the exchange unit formed by the gift of a woman and the counter-gift of a cannon. The movement of the exchange thus seems to be envisaged only from the standpoint of the return, as if the gift of the wife were secondary or were, rather, only relevant on a different level of value.

The three notions we have identified do not themselves provide a sufficient basis to construct hypotheses concerning the place of marriage exchanges in this society's value structure. They deal with marriage only in the narrow sense of the marriage ceremony, one limited aspect of the problem to be studied, and not with the entire inter-marriage relationship, reinforced as it is by the repeated transfer between 'houses' of all sorts of prestations. At Tanebar-Evav, two different expressions are used to describe prestations, depending on the direction in which they move. Those offered by the bridegroom's group to the bride's are designated by the general expression *flurut duad-nit*, while those moving in the opposite direction are called *fa'an fnólók*. The former expression means 'to let the *duad-nit* gorge themselves' (the *duad-nit*, 'the god–the dead', designates the bride's group). The latter may be translated 'to feed–to clothe'. Cannon, gongs and jewellery are offered in the first case, while plates and cloth are given in the second. These expressions indicate the existence of two contrary movements: one continuous flow toward 'the god–the dead', the other toward their uterine nephews. But while the first expression is used exclusively for the prestations of groups related by a prior marriage, the second is employed not only for prestations in the marriage relationship but also for those offered in relations of mutual aid or dependency. *Fa'an fnólók* thus implies a movement from a protector toward a person or group protected. Inter-marriage relationships consist of the ensemble of these two continuous movements in opposite directions, from the living to 'the god–the dead' and from the latter to the living through the intermediary of the mother's brother.

These movements may be fully understood only if placed in relation to the society's general system of values, which, for the moment, we can simply sketch. Two different words, *lór* and *haratut*, are used by the villagers to define their society and, at the same time, to express its two fundamental values. The combination *lór-haratut* signifies 'the society of Tanebar-Evav'. Each of the two words used separately refers to the society in relation to one of its two values. *Lór* is the society considered from the perspective of the law, which, in conjunction with certain spirits *mitu* who came from elsewhere, castigates murder, incest and adultery and intervenes when anything foreign – beneficial or harmful – arrives on the island, including the flotsam and jetsam which constantly wash ashore. The word also makes reference to a totality larger than Tanebar-Evav, composed of several villages under the authority of a single *raja*, the representative of this law. *Lór* thus incorporates a reference to other cultures.

Haratut is the society viewed from the standpoint of its relation with the Sun–Moon God (*duad ler vuan*), with the dead, with its mythical ancestors, with the sacred mountain in the centre of the island which, according to one myth, was the place of origin of both the society and money.[11] These two values, *lór* and *haratut*, indicate the simultaneous permeability and impermeability of Tanebar-Evav society, without however fixing a strict boundary between sea and land, outside and inside. They imply rather, in the case of *lór*, relations reaching out toward the surrounding world, and in the case of *haratut*, other relations turned toward the interior of the village. The society thus has two different and complementary manners of understanding its interdependent internal and external relations, as well as of incorporating in them the supernatural world. While certain other societies do not conceive of relations beyond their own universe, Tanebar-Evav, which often thinks in terms of 'containing' and 'contained', concerns itself as well with the passage in both directions from inside to outside and with the reciprocal relations uniting them. The combined reference to *lór-haratut* manifests the interplay in the society's ideology of these

11. There is actually no mountain. The villagers refer in this manner to the centre of the village, considered to be the centre of the world.

relations. Exchanges at Tanebar-Evav cannot be understood without reference to these two explicitly recognised values.

Our discussion of the three notions of 'ritual work', 'return' and 'replacement' demonstrates that, in terms of the vocabulary employed, exchanges of women cannot be distinguished from exchanges of goods, exchanges of murder, or even from exchanges between the living and supernatural beings. Further, these terms are not only employed in the case of exchanges between well-defined parties, the 'houses', but also in the context of ceremonial prestations which we might not at first sight have viewed as exchanges at all ('to bring up the ancestors in return', for example). The wide scope of these notions provides us with an image of what Tanebar-Evav society understands as exchange: ceremonial work consisting in the creation and renewal of relations between houses, or between the society and supernatural beings, with or without 'replacement', but in which the dominant obligation is the return. At Tanebar-Evav, a single prestation is simply one element in a constraining ensemble of permanent relations which maintain the individual actor in submission to something which transcends him completely.

It should be stressed, in conclusion, that while at Tanebar-Evav exchanges are seen as the task of creating and renewing relations, the vocabulary employed usually makes no direct reference to the society's values as such. The terms used describe the actions indispensable to the constant renewal of these values, but do not themselves offer a vision of the totality *lór-haratut*. Marriage exchanges cannot therefore be understood in isolation. One part of a broader intermarriage relationship, they must be placed in the context of the repeated, general movement, associated with the value *haratut*, which binds 'the god–the dead' to the living. At this level of value, and doubtless at that of *lór-haratut* as well, the relations in question extend beyond the sphere of exchanges, and their study permits us to attain an understanding of the society as a whole.

Iqar'iyen

The **Iqar'iyen** of the Moroccan Rif do not have a specific vocabulary for their exchanges, which nonetheless, in a sense, give its basic structure to this Berber society. These exchanges, furthermore, assume forms very different from those observed in Melanesia. Among the Orokaiva and the 'Are'are, in the absence of permanent groups, the exchanges themselves represent the active part of the social structure, and their analysis allows us to discover the societies' fundamental values. In the eastern Rif, on the contrary, the segmentary structure of tribal society is explicit, as are the values of honour and *baraka*. These data form the starting-point for a comprehension of the nature and primordial importance of exchanges in the society.

At first sight, both structure and values here call attention to certain entities, to permanent segmentary groups and to persons that are attributed or denied one of the two values. A member of the tribes is said to have or not to have honour; a descendant of the Prophet (a *sherif*, plural *shorfa*), is recognised as having or not having the divine blessing of *baraka*. On more careful examination, however, a description of social organisation stressing the importance of corporate groups proves inadequate, and exchange, though not spoken of in the society, must be brought into the analysis.

The structural relativity of segmentary groups has been stressed in the literature for quite some time. Nonetheless, the Arab proverb which sums up the rule governing this model – 'I against my brothers; my brothers and I against my cousins; my cousins, my brothers and I against everyone else' – invites us to place the rule itself in perspective. Indeed, confrontation and feuding in such a society are the very essence of the social structure. Violence here is not the negation of relation but, on the contrary, the form it necessarily assumes, while territorial limits and other sorts of separation between groups or persons appear, in a more fundamental sense, to be invitations to exchange.

Honour is a well-known feature of Mediterranean societies. It is usually described as a code of conduct for individuals, families and groups, all constantly exposed to the regard of public opinion. This form of honour exists among the Iqar'iyen. Every man of honour or group of honour exercises authority over a 'forbidden domain' or *haram*, embracing land, women, and houses, which must be preserved from scandal and defended against attack. However, the term *r'ird*, which we translate here as 'honour', has a verbal form with the connotations 'to invite' or 'to display ostentatiously', which incorporate an idea of challenge. It is unthinkable simply to defend one's honour passively. A man of honour

must seek out others like him, provoke them, challenge them to
act as he does. He must display his wealth and spend to the point
of ruin, forcing the person who receives from him to do the same.
Exchange is thus an essential aspect of honour. Two concepts come
into play here, *ettsh* 'to eat', a Berber term, and *qetl* 'to kill', a term
of Arabic origin. In the Rif and throughout Morocco, the verb 'to
eat' has two different senses. It signifies 'to consume', particularly
at feasts or during other ceremonies, but also 'to devastate', 'to
plunder', 'to ruin' a territory or a house, especially during a 'punitive expedition', *harka*. Used by a host and his guest, by an
aggressor and his victim, its underlying meaning never really
changes. By incurring expenses for a guest, by feeding him, 'giving him [something] to eat', one risks one's own ruin. A guest is
not just a friend whom one honours; he is also a rival seeking to
'plunder' his host and whom the latter challenges by feeding him,
by letting him try to ruin him. The Iqar'iyen say that they cannot
bear to see someone amass wealth. They seek to have a rich man
invite them to his table in great numbers, to oblige him to spend
what he has accumulated. They know, however, that once they
have received, they must give. 'To eat' at another's house, 'to eat'
another, sooner or later obliges one 'to offer [something] to eat' and
'to allow [oneself] to be eaten'. The same holds true for punitive
expeditions, since the destruction of another's goods is also an 'invitation' for him to do the same. In the definition of a man's identity, there is a close relationship between person and possessions.
Gift-giving is not, therefore, simply a question of emulation or a
peaceful means of exchange. It is a form of feuding which may lead
to the destruction of one or both parties.

The word *qetl* 'to kill' completes this idea of exchange of violence. The term signifies more precisely 'to give death' and thus
invites a return gift of the same nature. Reciprocity is here an essential principle of exchange, and a failure to reciprocate in kind
is considered proof of the partners' inequality in terms of honour.
Honour thus incorporates violence and killing ('the giving of
death') in the exchange system, and makes of exchanges of violence
the central form of social relations among the Iqar'iyen tribes.

Baraka or the 'divine blessing' is the relation uniting a man,
usually a *sherif*, to the omnipotent God of Islam. It is a gratuitous
gift, bestowed inexplicably, not as a reward for exemplary acts of
piety. A man of *baraka* has the capacity, in his vision of the universe
and in his acts, to transcend the human and social order. But he is

not simply a miracle worker, or an intercessor between God and man. He is also a non-violent mediator between men entangled in affairs of honour. In such cases, a *sherif*'s intervention opens the way to a very different form of exchange which, although beginning with a murder, concludes, for the time being, with the payment of a compensation called a *diyith*, 'blood money', to the victim's family. For Riffians, only a local saint has the power to put an end to exchanges of violence and re-establish the peace of God among the tribesmen. The two principal concepts pertinent here are *dbiha*, 'cutting the throat', and *hediya*, a 'present'. The former is the name given in the peace ritual *'ar*, presided over by a mediating *sherif*, to the sacrifice of a sheep, slaughtered in place of the murderer, who has first ritually offered himself as an expiatory victim. The animal's throat is cut with a knife, in accordance with Islamic canons. Once this sacrifice has been accomplished, further acts of vengeance are forbidden on pain of divine punishment. Like the term *qetl*, the word *dbiha* is at first sight neutral, since it contains no direct reference to values or to exchanges. The two words are, however, situated in totally different logics of exchange. *Qetl* is employed only in affairs of honour, while *dbiha*, on the contrary, is an escape from the constraints of honour, since the sacrifice, a manifestation of *baraka*, permits a human victim to be replaced by blood money.

An analogous conclusion may be reached from the use of the term *hediya*, a 'present'. Neutral also in appearance, since it is used to designate any present without regard to the circumstances in which it is offered, it describes here those given to the mediating *sherif* in gratitude for his services and, perhaps more important, in homage to his *baraka*. *Hediya* should be contrasted with *ettsh* 'to give [something] to eat'. The goods offered may be the same, but their significance is utterly different. 'To give [something] to eat' in an exchange of violence means not hesitating to ruin oneself for the sake of honour, but by giving one also obliges the beneficiary, an equal, to do the same. The presents offered by a man of honour to a *sherif*, that is, by a person of lower to one of higher status, do not call a return of the same nature. Rather, the *sherif* must succeed in his mediation, conduct the peace ritual and, through his *baraka*, make fertile the parties' forbidden domains. One cannot appropriately draw an equivalence here between the ritual services rendered and the goods offered, any more than between a human murder victim and the blood money offered in compensation for him.

Our study of Riffian vocabulary thus leads us to identify two contrasting forms of exchange. One, situated on the level of honour, supposes a reciprocity whose characteristics we describe in more detail below. The other permits a transition from murder to blood money through the intervention of an ultimate value, *baraka*, and takes us beyond reciprocity.

A reference to *baraka* transcends the sphere of exchanges, since this value defines a relation between men and the universal God of Islam, and is situated above society while also legitimating it. We shall see that the universal dimension of Islam, beyond exchange, proves to be decisive in a comparative analysis.

*

Our study of the terms and expressions used by these four societies to speak of their exchanges obliges us to detach ourselves from the usual modern terminologies, and suggests a few observations from a comparative perspective.

In none of the societies discussed does the vocabulary which differentiates the various forms of exchanges or expresses an idea of exchange offer an overall view of the society's system of exchanges. Among the Orokaiva the two words, *hande* and *pondo*, which seemingly define what is most essential in the society's exchanges, in fact describe only subsystems and omit any reference to the encompassing relation with the spirits. Among the 'Are'are and at Tanebar-Evav, terms are employed which refer to movements, partial operations, whose place in the society understood as a whole is left undefined. At Tanebar-Evav, these terms are supplemented by specific expressions, in marriage exchanges for example, which may only be fully understood when placed in relation with the values which organise the society as a totality. In the Rif, on the contrary, the terms used only take on meaning if reference is made from the first to the society's values which determine their orientation. In short, these societies never say 'exchange' but they practise it, if by 'exchanging' we understand repetition, return, replacement, 'linked succession', 'eating' and 'being eaten', sacrificing and working, all of which are only fragments that, in and of themselves, do not at first sight seem to compose a coherent system in any of the four.

The movements described in these vocabularies may be contrasted in two regards. The Orokaiva and the Iqar'iyen conceptualise a complete, outgoing and incoming, movement (challenge and counter-challenge, killing and being killed, *pondo* and *mine*), while expressing a notion of one-way movement on a different level, on a higher one (*hediya*) in the Rif and on the lowest one (*hande*) in the Papua New Guinean society. In both cases, a place is left for individual initiative, since, among the Orokaiva, an exchange sequence may be opened by creating a 'true reason' and, among the Iqar'iyen, by attacking one's neighbour without provocation. Nonetheless, placed in their overall context, these same events are subject to a different interpretation, since, for the Orokaiva, present exchanges give meaning to past events and at the same time close a sequence, while, in the Rif, an obligatory response may also be understood as the opening of other challenges and counter-challenges. On the contrary, among the 'Are'are and at Tanebar-Evav, the expressions employed describe only certain exchange operations presented essentially as returns, as if their original impulse were lost in the mists of time or, in any event, could simply be left unstated. For these two societies, an exchange is above all a response supposing the presence of a pre-existing order. The question may well be raised whether we are not in the presence here of an essential characteristic of all exchanges, and whether this element of return, which goes beyond individual initiative, is not indeed common to all four societies, since for the Orokaiva *amita be*, the 'true reason', gives an exchange a transcendent social meaning, expunging the event which was at its origin, and for the Iqar'iyen 'to eat' and 'to be eaten' are associated with an eminently social value, honour.

It is interesting that, in three of the societies discussed (1, 2 and 4), no words exist to designate the partners to an exchange, to define their position or their status in an exchange, or to refer to the individuals who take the initiative in exchanges. The terms never make reference to persons but rather to actions and movements or to prestations. The viewpoint (which nonetheless exists) of the individuals or of the partners does not seem to be determinative. At Tanebar-Evav (3), when speaking of a particular exchange the parties to it are named, but always together, as a pair (*yan ur-mang oho*), confirming that the pre-existing relationship between them takes precedence over the parties themselves.

Certain societies cannot speak of their exchanges without making express reference to a value system which is both abstract and concrete (*lór* and *haratut*, honour and *baraka*). Other societies, in contrast, speak exclusively of their exchanges themselves. Can it be concluded that the exchanges in the latter case are in a sense self-explanatory, that is, that they can be understood without reference to values which the societies themselves do not put into words? We attempt to demonstrate below that such societies' values are indeed implicit in and constitute 'the movement of the whole'. Our analysis of exchanges in these four societies will consequently be developed differently in each case to take into account the particularities of the data concerning them.

This brief foray into the exchange vocabularies of these four societies should cast light on the sort of comparative approach we envisage, as well as suggest the conditions of and limits to our endeavour. Comparison would indeed be only a dangerous illusion if, when we lent an ear to other societies, we were to insist on interposing the filter of current scientific terminology or to satisfy ourselves with comparing isolated parts of each society, torn from the whole which gives them meaning. It is our conviction that understanding can be achieved only by constant reference back to the totality of each society studied, and that only these totalities themselves may legitimately be compared. We attempt here to demonstrate in what terms such a comparison is possible.

Chapter 2

The Exchanges of Each Society Considered as a Whole

I: Orokaiva

Relations with the spirits

Before presenting a comprehensive synthesis of the Orokaiva exchange system, it is important to stress that for the Orokaiva the spirits of the dead participate directly in the society's exchanges. Only through their intervention can men obtain pork, the most vital element of exchanges among humans, whose acquisition is a constant, overriding concern.

The initiation ritual is said to be 'the most important part of custom' and 'the most exalted exchange, since pigs are slaughtered on the platform'. The ritual unfolds in three principal stages and affects the society as a whole, while at the same time settling the fate of children and pigs. It incorporates a double movement, renewing all the various sorts of relations among men through the exchange of pigs, and transforming children into subjects and pigs into objects of exchange.

The first stage (*jape*) of the ritual consists of a clash between men and spirits, provoked by an invitation to the spirits to enter the village. When they burst violently in, the distinction is shattered between village, abode of the living, and forest, where the spirits normally dwell. During this stage, everyone – initiated adults, guests and children – is successively placed in contact with the spirits. The constitutive distinctions of human society, among villages and among the inhabitants of a single village, are dissolved; only the distinction between men and spirits survives. Normal relations among men (wars, marriages, and exchanges of all sorts) are suspended; there remains only the confrontation between men and spirits, the common ancestors of all men. This pooling of ancestors is the clearest sign that all differentiation among men has been obliterated. The spirits seise hold of the children to be initiated, but are persuaded, by ritual means, to spare their lives. The first stage of the initiation is thus marked by the decomposition of society and the children's capture by the spirits.

During the second stage, the children are separated from the rest of society for several years and, confined in special houses in or near the village, are guarded by spirits in the guise of old men. The numerous prohibitions imposed on them during their reclusion are another sign that they remain in the spirits' power. Outside, on the contrary, intra-village relations among men, dissolved in the previous stage, flourish once again. Village society is gradually reestablished in a reconstructed space, as women resume their pig raising and men and women go back to work in their gardens.

In the third and final stage, the end of the candidates' reclusion is marked by a *pondo* ceremony in which men of different villages exchange both vegetable foodstuffs and pork. With the revival of inter-village exchanges, all the distinctions and relations among men, suppressed for a time, have thus been reconstituted and renewed by the action of the exchanges.

We cannot expose here in detail the society's complete itinerary as the initiation ritual unfolds.[12] It is, however, important to bear in mind that in the course of these ceremonies Orokaiva society traverses in turn and entirely renews each of the various sorts of relations of which it is composed. The initiation dissolves and then successively reconstitutes relations between men and spirits, among men within a village, and finally among various Orokaiva villages which will thereafter constitute a social universe.

The initiation renews the order of the world, capacitates children to participate in exchanges with spirits and men, and provides the society with the pigs it needs to continue its exchanges and to renew its relations. We know that the 'true reason' here is both pork and the children's 'social persons' – *hamo* – which the spirits have transformed and differentiated from pigs. The spirits thus grant children a credit of life which permits the latter to take part, as subjects, in exchanges among men. This credit expires when they finally die and join the spirits in the forest as spirits and pigs. The time that elapses between the opening of the credit by the separation of children and pigs, and its expiration when the dead go off

12. This analysis is set forth at length in a previously published monograph (Iteanu: 1983a).

into the forest, is for individual subjects the space of life itself, which only the unceasing repetition of the initiation ritual keeps open.

In the initiation, the various exchange relations form a coherent, hierarchically ordered totality in which each sort of relation has its own specific weight. In the monograph cited, we argue that relations with the spirits are situated at the highest hierarchical level and encompass all the others, conditioning their very existence. The following pages offer a brief synthesis of all the various Orokaiva exchange relations. We begin, in the next section, with a description of the *pondo* which closes the initiation ritual, a sequence the Orokaiva themselves consider typical. Then, in succeeding sections, we situate this exchange in the context of the full initiation ritual, and compare initiation with the marriage and funeral rituals.

The *pondo* for the decoration of children

In this section we describe a specific but highly characteristic exchange, the *pondo* which concludes the initiation ritual. This exchange is part of an elaborate ceremony during which the children, who now emerge from their long period of reclusion (from three to seven years), are decorated.

Some time after a candidate begins his reclusion, his parents select the person who is to prepare his ornaments.[13] For the first child initiated, who is usually the oldest sibling, a relative on his mother's side is chosen; for the second, a relative on his father's mother's side; and for the third, another relative on his father's side, but not from his father's mother's side. The principal partners to this *pondo* exchange are the child's father and his decorator. The latter almost always comes from another village.

While the ornaments are being prepared, a process which usually takes several months, a large, high ceremonial platform is constructed in the centre of the village. The pillars to which it is attached are uprooted *popo* trees, inverted and driven into the ground. Each represents one of the pigs to be slaughtered in the course of the ceremony. If a pig has long tusks, the roots of the

---

13. Although a candidate may be male or female and may have more than one decorator, in the following paragraphs, for simplicity's sake, we describe the case of a male candidate with a single decorator.

corresponding tree are carved to resemble two huge tusks which overhang the platform. On the late afternoon of the day before the children's reclusion ends, all those who have taken part in the preparation of the *pondo* gather in the village – the parents of the children to be initiated, those who helped assemble the vegetable foodstuffs for the following day's offerings, those who worked on the construction of the platform and, finally, those who are to participate in the children's decoration. For the occasion, the women cook great quantities of food which are exchanged among the houses of the village; this 'women's food' marks a ritual sequence where the women's role is preponderant. Far into the night those present sing and beat on drums, tell stories, and chew large quantities of areca-nuts and betel leaves.

Shortly before dawn, the women take the candidates from their houses of reclusion to a nearby stream where they now once again have the right to bathe themselves. They are then led into the forest, where for hours, in secretly prepared clearings, they are adorned with ornaments made of feathers, seashells and dogteeth. Only late in the afternoon do the magnificently adorned children make their entry into the village, preceded by those who decorated them and followed by dancers. The domesticated pigs which return to the village at the same hour for their nightly feeding are seized and hobbled, then gently placed on pieces of fragile barkcloth to await slaughter. The women and children remain at their side, wailing and lamenting endlessly. They weep for these pigs which for long years have been 'their children' or 'their brothers'.

It is then that the *pondo* exchanges begin. A candidate's father offers taros and pork principally to his child's decorator, but also to everyone else who, in one way or another, has contributed to his child's upbringing and initiation. The taros which were heaped on the platform the day before are now disposed at its foot in piles, each of which is intended for a specific recipient. The pigs are hoisted onto the platform, killed with a spear and carved up. Each pig's owner calls out successively the names of the persons to whom he offers some pork, proclaiming at the same time the 'true reason' – *amita be* – for the gift. (In the case of a decorator, for example, the father's 'true reason' is the adornment of his child.) After each name, the donor descends rapidly from the platform and places the piece of pork on top of its recipient's taro pile. The donee then stands up, his gifts are gathered up by the women and adolescents accompanying him, and this whole group returns straightway to its village with him in the lead.

Once the decorators and other invited guests have received their offerings, the donors throw the remaining pieces of pork from the platform to those who attend the feast without a specific invitation. Whoever is struck by one of these projectiles may keep it for himself. Since both invited and uninvited visitors from other villages leave as soon as they have received some pork, soon only village residents remain.

When the decorators first arrive in the village before the *pondo*, they offer a small quantity of foodstuffs, a prestation called *tihanga*, to their prospective *pondo* donors. The latter consume it now, after all the non-residents have departed. Indeed, in theory, they have nothing else left to eat, since all their own foodstuffs should have been distributed at the feast.

The food received by the donees at the *pondo* is itself redistributed by them. Once the decorators, for example, have regained their villages, they share out what they have received among their relatives, neighbours, and others who helped them prepare their participation in the *pondo*. The decorator and his immediate family are finally left with just a few taros and a small piece of pork fat. The young men of the decorators' villages go from house to house eating bits of pork and then, taking advantage of the night, go off to their lovers' trysts.

Some time after the initiation *pondo*, each decorator must offer his donor, the father of the child he adorned, a prestation *mine* identical to what he himself received. At a ceremony called *pondo mine*, he returns to the father the same sorts and quantities of food that the latter had solemnly distributed to him at the *pondo*. If the partners live in the same village, which is rare in the case of initiation but quite frequent in other *pondo* exchanges, the return *mine* should be offered immediately. Otherwise, the time which elapses may be longer, and depends in part on the quantity of food distributed initially; the smaller it was, the sooner it will be returned.

At the *mine* ceremony the father, for his part, offers the decorator a *tihanga* corresponding to the one he himself received at the initiation, and also gives back to him the feathers and other ornaments which constituted the child's adornment.

The decorator, who shared out almost everything he received in the *pondo* among his neighbours and friends, receives assistance from them when the time comes for him to offer the *mine*. The father, who received substantial aid for the *pondo* from his neighbours and friends, must offer prestations to all of them as soon as the decorator offers him the *mine*, redistributing to them almost everything he receives.

The exchanges between the father or the decorator on the one hand and their respective helpers on the other are *hande* exchanges which do not balance exactly. Indeed, father and decorator should normally offer their assistants more food than they have received or will receive from them, since they redistribute, in addition, the equivalent of their own contributions. Inasmuch as the father and decorator alone offer live pigs, their helpers, who furnish only vegetable foodstuffs, also receive a greater variety of food than what they give. Helpers who contribute labour rather than food must also receive something, and most village young people get small gifts as well. The father's helpers, furthermore, may offer him at the *pondo* more food than he has 'true reasons' to give away. He will then distribute this surplus to recipients who may never return it (young people, for example), or he may just let it spoil. Nonetheless, in either event, at the *mine* he will have to offer something to the helpers who gave it to him. The decorator, for his part, when the time comes for him to offer the *mine*, will surely not be able to recover everything he distributed after the *pondo*, and will have to make up the difference himself.[14]

The father at the *pondo* should, supposedly, distribute everything he owns, his pigs and the produce of his gardens, among all the guests, and the decorator at the *mine* should do the same. Further, for a feast to be considered a success it is not enough for the donor to have satisfied his friends in exchange-related matters. They must also have enjoyed the superb dances, admired the dancers' splendid costumes, and generally have spent an agreeable day.

If a feast-giver produces sufficient food to satisfy everyone, he proves that he is a good exchange partner *pondo embo* and, furthermore, a generous man *hande embo*. If the food he provides is insufficient, he is neither a generous man nor a wise one *kiari embo*; in short, he is not a serious exchange partner. In the case of the *mine*, although the decorator has the primary responsibility for providing the food, the father remains responsible to his former helpers for giving them as much or more than what they contributed at the *pondo*. If he obtains insufficient return prestations from the decorator, it means that he was unable to come to an understand-

14. Both father and decorator are, in addition, obliged to assist in turn their helpers when the latter offer feasts.

ing with him, or simply that he has let himself be taken advantage of. In either case, doubt is cast on his capacity as a feast-giver.

The initiation *pondo* and its mandatory *pondo mine* thus seem, at first sight, to form a coherent unit in an exchange system founded on strict reciprocity. This impression is misleading, but results unavoidably from having to isolate temporarily, for the purposes of analysis, a single link in what is in reality a chain of exchanges. When these ceremonies are reintegrated in the complete Orokaiva ritual cycle, a very different vision of the overall system of prestations emerges. In the following parts we discuss the three principal stages of this cycle: initiation, marriage and funerals.

Initiation exchanges

When the *pondo* for the adornment of children and its corresponding *mine* are placed in the broader context of the entire initiation ritual, they are seen to be the final stage in a sequence of ceremonies. The full initiation includes three principal stages. In the first, called *jape*, the spirits of the dead, portrayed by the candidates' relatives as well as certain other co-villagers and inhabitants of surrounding villages, invade the candidates' village. They carry out their assault to the sound of three sorts of secret musical instruments – flutes *sepiripa*, bull-roarers *umbuvupa* and nut-shell whistles *kornipamone* – which are always kept hidden from the uninitiated. This terrifying music is said to be the voices of the spirits, who attack the children, damage houses, uproot palm trees, kill domesticated pigs, visit unsightly deformities on transgressors of initiation prohibitions and corrupt the relations between brothers and between husband and wife which are fundamental to village life. After several hours of depredations, the spirits are placated by a prestation called *ji be torari*, 'the gathering of wild fruits from the trees', composed of wild game and wild fruits. This offering is unilateral, that is, is not matched by any return *mine*. Once the spirits receive it, they 'put their voices away' and leave the village.

The spirits thus agree to spare the children, to take them in charge and to assure their differentiation from pigs. The *ji be torari* would seem to be offered to the spirits in place of the children they have seized, in exchange for the credit of life granted them. This prestation, composed of forest products and offered to forest spirits, suggesting identity, allows men to exchange among themselves something 'other', pigs instead of men. The spirits accept this prestation only temporarily of course. They will receive their real return offering piecemeal, on each child's death, when his corpse is transformed into various wild animals which return to the forest. In the interval, the ritual has established a distinction between children and pigs, enabling men to exchange the latter at their *pondo*.

Only this preliminary agreement makes possible the *pondo* for the adornment of children, which follows on their long reclusion and finally ratifies the definitive separation of their fate from that of pigs. This *pondo* has a 'true reason', since it marks considerable transformations in the children's social persons – *hamo* – and since the offerings made there consist principally of pork. The return of the 'true reason' at the *mine* relegates the exchange to a definitively completed past, sheltered from human judgement and proof against men's wiles. Once the return prestation has been offered, an exchange, like the actions of the spirits themselves, may no longer be called into question, since its 'reason' has been expunged by the return and complete consumption of the pork.

At a lower level, the helpers *aka* contribute vegetable foodstuffs, and the young men and numerous other guests revel and dance at the expense of the feast-givers. Here, it is a question of *hande* prestations, for which no identical return *mine* is required. There is no expunging of the past and no 'true reason'; the partners' 'inside' *jo* simply finds spontaneous expression in giving. Although the helpers receive what, from our viewpoint, would seem to be return prestations, the Orokaiva do not perceive them as such, since they are not exactly equal to the original prestations offered. As explained above, they are indeed usually larger, though they may occasionally be smaller.

The hierarchical relation between these two levels of exchange, *pondo* and *hande*, is confirmed by the fact that pork offered at a *pondo* later nourishes interpersonal *hande* relations when it is redistributed, but a piece of pork which has already circulated in a *hande* exchange may never reascend onto the platform in a *pondo* exchange. Thus, while the pork from a *pondo*, smoked for conservation, is sometimes later offered in other ceremonies, it may only circulate there at ground level, and is always considered inferior to pork freshly killed on the platform. Further corroboration that pork which descends from the platform passes irremediably from a higher to a lower level of value is provided by the Orokaivas' marked preference for pork fat which is never smoked and conserved.

To sum up, initiation exchanges involve, first of all, a level at which a prestation is offered specifically to the spirits, to stave them off temporarily. This offering finds its place in the framework of the encompassing exchange between spirits and men, which is only closed for each person at his burial. Next, at the *pondo* level, the exchanges of pork and vegetable foodstuffs bind the candidates' families to those of their decorators. Pork is here the tangible aspect of the 'true reason', and its distribution from the platform at the *pondo mine* definitively ratifies the transformations in the candidates' *hamo*. Finally, at the *hande* level, individual subjects allow their 'inside' *jo* to speak, expressing their generosity in gifts of vegetable foodstuffs and pork which has already descended from the platform. While *pondo* exchanges are clearly situated on a higher level than *hande* exchanges, the hierarchical position of the prestation offered to the spirits *ji be torari* can only be fixed after an analysis of Orokaiva marriage and funeral rituals.

Marriage exchanges

In the marriage ritual, as in the initiation ritual, a first level of exchange may be distinguished. After the groom comes in the dark of night to carry off his future bride, in the early morning her parents discover her disappearance. They immediately muster their relatives, in particular those on her mother's side, who are charged with discovering as quickly as possible what has happened to her. The troop of the bride's relatives starts off forthwith to look for her. When they arrive in the groom's village, they set about damaging the houses and bullying and insulting the inhabitants. The assailants behave quite like the spirits when they ransack a village during the first stage of the initiation ritual. As a condition for stopping the destruction, the bride's relatives demand numerous gifts, collectively called *o sobu* 'the pig [for having wet one's feet in] the morning dew'. These prestations do not however necessarily consist of pigs, since each of the bride's relatives may request for himself whatever he wishes. They are presented by the bridegroom's relatives principally to affines of affines, and thus recall that the bride's mother circulated from affines of affines to affines. They create a certain solidarity between affines of affines, affines and wife-takers. As soon as the bride's mother's relatives are satisfied, they convey the bride's parents' demands, listing down to the smallest detail all the things claimed as marriage prestations. Once agreement on these is reached, the first phase of the ritual is at an end.

The prestation *o sobu* is strangely reminiscent of the offering *ji be torari* made during the first stage of the initiation ritual. Both are unilateral. While the *ji be torari* in the *jape* ceremony staves off the spirits, who want to carry off the initiation candidates, the *o sobu* staves off the bride's mother's relatives, who behave like spirits and want to seize the bride and take her back. Composed of various objects collectively called a 'pig', the *o sobu* represents a payment for the service the wife-givers' affines render to both parties by their willingness to accept the bride's equivalence with the pig or pigs that her parents will later receive. Unlike the *jape* ceremony, however, only affines intervene here, not the spirits themselves. This diminished appearance of the spirits is one sign of the subordination of the marriage ritual to the initiation ritual.

Sometime thereafter, the marriage prestations, *a dorobu*, decided on in the previous stage, are offered to the bride's parents. They always include at least one pig, substantial quantities of vegetable foodstuffs (especially taros), splendid feather and seashell ornaments, bark-cloth, string bags and clay pots. The Orokaiva say that the pig is the bride's 'social person' – *hamo* – or her 'fat', which her parents may not consume themselves, since they would be 'eating their own daughter's *hamo*'. The food offered is entirely redistributed to those who had a part in the 'constitution of the bride's *hamo*', we would say, in her upbringing. Feathers and shells are generally associated with the 'images of the dead', *ahihi*, that is, with the spirits of the forest, the third element which, together with *hamo* and *jo*, makes up the total Orokaiva person.

With this prestation, the marriage ritual comes to an end. Henceforth relations between affines, like those between men and spirits, are marked by the greatest respect and are subject to numerous prohibitions. The bride's parents thus receive a pig in return for their daughter. However, since the initiation ritual formerly introduced a distinction between children and pigs, the bride is no longer identical to a pig, and the marriage ritual must be performed to change her status so that a pig may be accepted in replacement for her. On the level of the encompassing exchange with the spirits, opened at the beginning of the initiation ritual, the exchange of their daughter for a pig is, for the bride's parents, a sort of partial closing of the life credit conceded her by the spirits at her initiation. However, as we shall see below, a person's life credit, whatever his or her sex, only expires definitively at his or her funeral.

It should be stressed that the feather and shell ornaments of the *a dorobu* circulate only in one direction, from wife-takers to wife-givers. While at the initiation *pondo* the bride's brother uses these ornaments to decorate his uterine nephew or niece, and then receives them back at the *pondo mine*, they do not, strictly speaking, form part of either exchange. At the *mine*, identical but different pigs and taros are returned for those initially offered. On the contrary, the very same ornaments that were used for the child's decoration at the *pondo* are later given back at the *mine*, reverting to the place where the previous generation of wife-takers had conveyed them. From the Orokaiva viewpoint, this loan is a sort of ritual service which does not constitute a *pondo* exchange. The feathers and shells thus follow a one-way path along a vector from wife-takers to wife-givers, that is, toward the persons who represent the spirits, deviating from it only momentarily when they are lent for the decoration of a nephew or a niece.

The feathers and shells received by a brother at his sister's marriage will be used by him to decorate his uterine nephew or niece at the initiation *pondo*, and the ornaments of the initiation *pondo* announce the feathers and shells to be offered or received on the occasion of a candidate's marriage. In this regard, the two rituals seem, at first sight, to manifest a certain symmetry. However, the brother–sister link, vital to the initiation of a married couple's children, is permanent. Despite the marriage ritual, it continues uninterrupted, reaffirmed in its modified form by the circulation of feathers and shells. The affinity relationships arising from a marriage, on the contrary, do not outlast the marriage itself. An enduring cross-sex sibling relationship thus encompasses more unstable affinity. The ornaments of the marriage prestation, turned toward the initiation, are another sign of the subordination of marriage in the ritual cycle.

Funeral exchanges

The funeral ritual follows essentially the same pattern as initiation and marriage. During an initial stage, the inhabitants of the deceased's village, as well as his relatives and friends living in other villages, gather to weep over him. During the funeral vigil, the mourners conduct themselves strangely, in ways which recall the spirits, and only gradually abandon their odd behaviour as dirge follows dirge through the long night. At dawn, the deceased's relatives cook food and offer it to the mourners to induce them to put an end to their lamentations. This prestation, called *si ta indari* 'food for the tears [shed]', is not matched by a corresponding *mine*. The first part of the funeral ritual comes to an end with the burial of the corpse, whose humours are said to turn into pigs and other forest animals. Like the initiation and marriage rituals, the funeral ritual thus begins with a unilateral prestation offered to placate persons behaving like spirits, which opens the way to subsequent *pondo* level exchanges between men and villages.

First, however, the widow goes into seclusion in the house beneath which her husband is buried, and remains there for several months during which she weaves the mourning vest *baja*. When, at the end of this period, her brother offers her late husband's relatives a *pondo* consisting of a pig and taros, she drapes the pig in this vest, which represents the deceased's 'image' *ahihi*. Thereafter, the widow ends her retreat and, if she likes, may return to live with her family or remarry.

The *pondo* that the widow's brother offers her late husband's relatives may be considered the return prestation for the *a dorobu* offered at the time of the marriage. Unlike the children's decoration ceremony, which includes both a *pondo* and its corresponding *mine*, the pigs and taros of the marriage prestations are only returned to the husband's relatives by his wife's at his funeral.[15] This return of the prestations offered at marriage would seem to be the closing and filing away at the *pondo* level of the relations between affines.

The encompassing exchange with the spirits, inaugurated for a given generation at the initiation ceremony, closes for a particular

---

15. All funerals do not unfold in precisely the same manner. They vary depending, among other things, on which spouse dies first, how many children the couple has had, the composition of the extended family, and the cause of death. We present here a rather simple case to demonstrate the general principles at work in the ritual.

person when, after burial, the temporary distinction between men and pigs to which the spirits had consented at the initiation is abolished in his case. Later, when the widow drapes the pig of the funeral *pondo* in the mourning vest, she puts an end to the marriage. For each man, his funeral is thus a sort of double closing, at the encompassing level of the exchange with the spirits and at the *pondo* level of exchanges among men.

The scope of the funeral ritual is narrower than that of initiation or marriage, since it concerns only the deceased and those who had personal contact with him. On the contrary, initiation opens and renews the encompassing exchange with the spirits for the society as a whole, and marriage involves groups of affines as such.

Initiation, marriage and funeral prestations are all summarised graphically in Chart 1. If inter-individual *hande* prestations are taken into account as well, three levels of exchange may be distinguished. In each ritual, the first level, that of the exchange with the spirits, is superior in value to the other two, since it determines the status of the distinction between subjects and objects. On this highest level, during the indispensable first stage of the initiation, marriage and funeral rituals, prestations are always offered unilaterally by men to the spirits or those who represent them. This exchange is opened for each generation of children, but also and more fundamentally for the whole society, when the spirits agree to differentiate between children and pigs, conceding a life credit to the former and leaving the latter at the disposal of men for their *pondo* exchanges. The three prestations at this level are all oriented along the same vector toward the spirits, indicating that in each case the same fundamental task of defining the relations between men and pigs is taken up again. At initiation, the spirits themselves are invoked to separate children and pigs; in the marriage ritual, the wife-givers' affines, in the context of inter-village relations, must accept the partial equivalence of pigs and women; finally, the mourners, in the context of inter-individual relations, accompany the deceased during his corpse's definitive transformation into wild animals.

Three dimensions may thus be distinguished in the ritual cycle: first, a movement from collective initiation to individual death; second, a hierarchical relationship between the initiation ritual in its completeness and the marriage and funeral rituals, whose prestations taken together resemble those of the initiation ritual; and, finally, a movement within each ritual from relations between

men and spirits to relations between villages (*pondo*) and finally
to those between individual subjects (*hande*).

*

Once these three levels of exchange have been identified, the entire Orokaiva ritual cycle reveals itself to be a coherent whole,
whose analysis opens the way to an understanding of the fundamental values governing the society. Going beyond the simple differentiation and description of several patterns of exchanging
goods, the problem becomes to elucidate the relative position of
each kind of exchange in the society's hierarchy of values.

Each Orokaiva ritual is indeed composed of two different sorts
of activity. On the one hand, there is the ritual strictly speaking,
whose rigid forms, rooted in the ancestors' teachings, may in no
way be tampered with by men. For the Orokaiva, regular repetition of the rituals received from their ancestors is the means of
remaining in contact with them. Ritual, not genealogy, is here the
tie between the living and the ancestors (Iteanu: 1983b). On the
other hand, there are the prestations of foodstuffs and other objects which, at each of the rituals, are the specific contribution of
the living. The quantity of goods offered, the beauty of their presentation and the donor's alacrity in giving them are an expression
of his personal worth and generosity.

In the first stage of initiation, marriages and funerals, ritual
conduct has more value than gifts of food. On this level of exchange, fixed repetitive actions occupy a hierarchically superior
position and permit the modification of the relations between men
and pigs.

In the second stage of all three rituals, ritual conduct is subordinated to *pondo* exchanges where the prestations of pigs render
'true' and tangible the transformations operated during the first
stage. The *mine*, 'perfect repetition' of the initial prestations, is simply a subordinated form of the more fundamental repetition observed in the first stage of each ritual. In an exchange of goods, how
better indeed to suggest the idea of repetition than by returning
precisely the same quantities of precisely the same things of precisely the same size? The reciprocity a Western observer perceives
here is, for the Orokaiva, not a primary value, but simply a subordinated form of their most fundamental value, repetition of the
rituals.

CHART 1

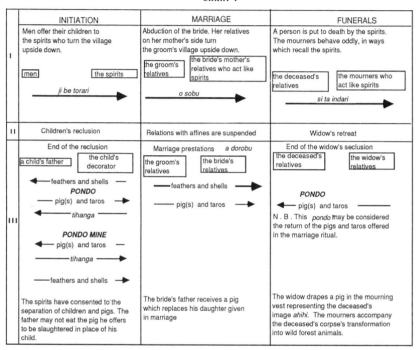

	INITIATION	MARRIAGE	FUNERALS
I	Men offer their children to the spirits who turn the village upside down. men → the spirits *ji be torari* →	Abduction of the bride. Her relatives on her mother's side turn the groom's village upside down. the groom's relatives → the bride's mother's relatives who act like spirits *o sobu* →	A person is put to death by the spirits. The mourners behave oddly, in ways which recall the spirits. the deceased's relatives → the mourners who act like spirits *si ta indari* →
II	Children's reclusion	Relations with affines are suspended	Widow's retreat
III	End of the reclusion a child's father → the child's decorator ← feathers and shells — ***PONDO*** — pig(s) and taros → ← *tihanga* — ***PONDO MINE*** ← pig(s) and taros — — *tihanga* → — feathers and shells → The spirits have consented to the separation of children and pigs. The father may not eat the pig he offers to be slaughtered in place of his child.	Marriage prestations *a dorobu* the groom's relatives → the bride's relatives — feathers and shells → — pig(s) and taros → The bride's father receives a pig which replaces his daughter given in marriage	End of the widow's seclusion the deceased's relatives → the widow's relatives ***PONDO*** ← pig(s) and taros — N.B. This *pondo* may be considered the return of the pigs and taros offered in the marriage ritual. The widow drapes a pig in the mourning vest representing the deceased's image *ahihi*. The mourners accompany the deceased's corpse's transformation into wild forest animals.

The Roman numerals I, II and III indicate the three stages of each ritual.
Prestations for which there is no corresponding return prestation are represented by boldface arrows.
Prestations for which a corresponding return prestation is offered are represented by lightface arrows.

Finally, at the *hande* level, the principles governing ritual activity and *pondo* exchanges have lesser importance. The field is left open for the forces located in the 'inside' *jo* to express themselves through the individual subject.

II: 'Are'are

'Are'are exchanges order all the society's activities, to the point that it is often difficult to draw the Western distinction between daily and ceremonial life. In the course of these exchanges, we observe the movement of 'things', among which are numbered living persons, the corpses of murder victims, pigs, taros and, most important of all, money. This last usually consists of strands of shell-beads strung in varying lengths. The standard unit measures a fathom and contains twenty-four units of fifty beads each, or one thousand two hundred beads in all. This money is divisible and serves as a measuring rod, situating on a single scale events as different as the purchase of ten taros or of a canoe, a marriage or a murder, the amount of a funeral prestation, the payment for a ritual service or for an ensemble of musicians, and the monetary pledge which gives a social sanction to flirtation. The translation of an event into monetary terms is a sort of seal which makes it official by giving it definitive meaning and weight.

The universality of 'Are'are exchanges makes it imperative in describing and interpreting them, and consequently in giving an overall view of the society, not to dissociate the various, intertwined ceremonies – marriages, payments of blood money, funerals and 'big men's' feasts. In what follows, we have attempted rather to distinguish the various types of prestations within this ceremonial ensemble, and to determine in each case the effect they have on three spheres which, as a first approximation, we may define as relations between persons, relations between groups and, finally, the relations of a socio-cosmic nature between the living and the dead.

The ascending monetary prestations of the funeral feast

These prestations are offered by persons who arrive in a long single file, and each give the grave-digger a strand of money no more than a fathom long. These strands are attached to a horizontal pole set above a ceremonial platform constructed in the middle of a mortuary village specially built on the deceased's land. The platform serves as a means to display the money presented at the feast, both when it is handed up and later when it is handed down. Two or three years later, this money is returned by the deceased's family to the men, women and children, who offer it at the 'return funeral feast'. In the meantime, the grave-digger lends the strands to those who helped him assemble the pigs and taros he furnished for the feast, to which his contribution of food precisely equals that made by the deceased's family. A monetary loan of this sort binds the lenders both to the grave-digger and to the deceased's descendants.

From the inter-personal standpoint, the offering made by each guest at the feast is almost certainly the continuation of a previously established binary relationship with the deceased, though in appearance it takes the form of a spontaneous initiative. It has the further effect of opening a credit in favour of the person who presents it to the grave-digger. This credit is added to all the other offerings of the same kind that the donor made in previous years and which were then suspended from the poles above other funeral platforms. In a system where hoarding is reputed to be perilous, since money brings illness and even death, the strands of money offered constitute for each lender a sort of circulating monetary credit which comes back to him in small amounts at each return funeral feast.

From the inter-group standpoint, the prestations offered by different individuals to the grave-digger represent a substantial contribution to 'the work of mourning' group assembled around him. Indeed, this group benefits from this loan for the time it needs to permit it to reconstitute the gardens and stocks of pigs it drew upon for the feast. The loan also sometimes prolongs the cohesion of the group, which may properly be called ceremonial since it is formed only for a particular funeral. It is composed in part of the grave-digger's relatives and friends, in part of other persons who, at the proper moment, had pigs and taros available that they wished to convert into money. This may also be the occasion for the 'work of mourning' group to acknowledge the *savoir faire* of a 'big man', the grave-digger, whom they would do well to live near. In a completely different manner, these prestations also concern 'the roots of the feast', the group assembled around the deceased's family, which shares responsibility for the ceremony with the 'work of mourning' group, since the offerings in question increase their prestige by giving greater lustre to the feast.

Finally, from the standpoint of 'Are'are society as a whole or, more precisely, of the society in its relation with the universe, all these 'ascending' prestations, offered on the day of the deceased's commemorative funeral feast by a large number of different persons, compose, in exclusively monetary form, his 'image', that is, the deceased in his greatest glory, transformed into an ancestor.[16] The total sum which has been handed up to the platform is proclaimed. The greater it is, the greater will be the ancestor's influence over his descendants, for good or for ill. The transfer over time of these strands of money from one funeral platform to another is thus the circulation of the 'ancestor-images' of the entire society. An image on the day of its splendour is composed of strands of money made of shell-beads which have already been presented at prior funeral feasts and which will later contribute to the formation of future ancestor-images at subsequent funeral feasts. This constant movement of ancestor-images, the earlier ones fragmenting and rejoining to form new ones, is the great task of the whole society and of each of its members.

In this movement from platform to platform, every person has on deposit a credit balance which no one else can touch. The credits a lender concedes are eventually always paid back, either to him or, in the event of his death, to his children. They are indeed simply fragments of ancestor-images which, taken together, foreshadow the contours of his own future ancestor-image. At the same time they represent, in tangible form, the ultimate value of 'Are'are society, its money – its ancestors.

---

16. The 'Are'are consider the living person to be constituted of a temporary association of three elements essential to the conduct of his activities: 'body' *rape*, 'breath' *manomano*, and 'image' *nunu*. 'Body' consists of flesh, bone, and various humours. 'Breath' manifests itself not only in respiration but also in the pulsing of the blood and the ejaculation of sperm. 'Image', finally, is associated with a person's name. 'Body', 'breath' and 'image' are also considered to be the constituent elements of the universe and are ordered among themselves in a hierarchy in which 'image' encompasses both breath and body. An 'image' is an ancestor, and shell-money is 'ancestor-image'.

The ascending monetary prestations of the 'big man's' feast[17]

These prestations consist of small sums of money which have previously been offered to unmarried men by unmarried young women during ceremonial flirtations which unfold over an eight-month period. In the ninth month, the preannounced 'big man's' feast takes place. Participation is restricted to men, married or unmarried, associated with various Panpipe ensembles. The money received in the flirtations is handed up by the unmarried men to the platform, where it is counted. The total, publicly proclaimed, is the measure of the 'big man's' renown. The money is then returned to the unmarried men, who later return it to the young women.

From the interpersonal standpoint, these monetary prestations ratify the secret lovers' trysts in the forest, reveal how many amorous adventures each unmarried man has had, and sometimes permit the establishment of lasting sentimental attachments which lead to marriage if they are made public. The girls obtain their money by selling tubers from their gardens or pigs they have raised. The number of their suitors is proof both of their personal charms and of the prosperity of their undertakings. The unmarried men offer them in exchange objects such as combs, knives, tobacco, pipes or pieces of cloth, which are not returned.

These monetary prestations also have a significance transcending the personal context, however, since their total, when it is proclaimed, testifies to the success of the feast, that is, to the vigour both of the group supporting the 'big man's' efforts and of the Panpipe ensembles that have played their music with brio and flamboyantly offered the money from their trysts.

Each Panpipe ensemble, carrying a forest of leafy branches and in a state of great excitement, accompanies the money it has collected to the foot of the platform. The ceremony does not simply end there, however, but takes a rather surprising turn, as the men begin to burlesque each other's failings, exchanging with impunity the coarsest insults and aping frenetic and scandalous couplings. In the evening, after a meal of taro cakes, the guests on their

17. A person may be recognized as a 'big man' *mane paina* in one of two ways, either as a 'killer' *namo* or, on the contrary, as a 'peace-master' *aaraha*. A peace-master, however, represents a value so much higher, both in renown and in the ranking of the rituals, that, other than in the context of the relation between killers and peace-masters, 'big man' means essentially 'peace-master'. A 'big man's' feast is always offered by a 'peace-master', who may only do so after he has already given the funeral feasts of his father, his mother and his mother's brother.

way home destroy the gardens and coconut palms of the 'big man',
who utters not a word in protest. He accepts this destruction eq-
uably and, in consequence, his prestige, as well as that of those
associated with him, increases. At the same time, the possibility
of his offering another feast is postponed for many years. Rare were
the 'big men' who could offer more than two feasts in their lifetime, so costly is their glory and so complete their ruin. For a 'big
man', the honours of his feast are thus quite ambiguous, since the
Panpipe ensembles and the men associated with them commit acts
which are at the very least disrespectful and some of which are
frankly destructive.

From the standpoint of the society in its socio-cosmic dimension, the bundles of money from the ceremonial flirtations appear
to be images, not of ancestors (that is, of those who died of illness),
but rather of 'murder victims', the other category of the dead,
which includes the victims of true murders as well as suicides,
women who have died in childbirth and stillborn fetuses. 'Murder victims' are not given burial and never attain the status of ancestors. Their bodies are left to rot on the floor of the forest, the
only place where lovers' trysts take place. At each 'big man's' feast,
murder victims make an appearance in the form of the bundles of
money presented and raised up to the high platform by the unmarried men of the Panpipe groups. These bundles, called 'the children of the bamboo' (that is, of the music),[18] are, in this feast of the
ninth month, like stillborn fetuses parodying the real births which
result from marriage. Next to the platform, a high display stand
called the 'murder victims' stand' is erected. Strings of taros and
coconuts, the vegetable foodstuffs for the feast, are coiled about
its rungs, in the same way that a murder victim's body is sometimes attached to a horizontal wooden pole and offered to a prior
victim's family. Thus, the very things which give lustre to the 'big
man's' feast, the money and the food to be consumed, bear the
murder victims' mark. The money, counted and proclaimed on the
platform, constitutes an ironic presentation of the 'big man's' social stature and his image at the peak of his renown. His glory is
composed of the images of anonymous murder victims which
come, like a living reproach, to spread the bitter taste of mockery.
These murder victims have quite diverse origins. Some recall the
well-known fact that no one can become a 'big man', that is, a

---

18. In the language of the 'Are'are, the same word, *'au*, means both 'bamboo' and 'music'.

'peace-master', without having for years first been a 'killer', constantly lying in wait for persons with a price on their head, and unable to assure the prosperity of his own entourage or to raise a family. Other murder victims recall that, even after becoming the peace-master of a 'territorial canoe' (a territory),[19] a 'big man' often cannot protect his 'canoe' and its inhabitants from the murderous attacks of killers coming from beyond its borders.

Furthermore, right in the middle of one 'big man's' feast, other 'big men' begin proudly to announce the forthcoming feasts which they will soon be giving. The money of the present feast, after having been returned to the girls, will later constitute the images of other 'big men' at their feasts. The circulation of the money deriving from ceremonial flirtations – that is, of the murder victims' images – feeds on preceding feasts and contributes to the success of future ones. A 'big man's' glory on the day of his feast is composed of monetary fragments of past feasts which will later furnish the material for other 'big men's' renown in the future. The lovely staging of this money's ascent to the platform thus seems meant to parody the circulation of ancestor-images at funeral feasts, and a 'big man' himself appears to be simply a sort of caricature of an ancestor. 'Big men', whatever glory they may achieve, can never attain the fundamental value of the ancestors. Their attempts to do so leave them caught up in the untimely parade of the murder victims, which draws upon the small sums resulting from barren caresses. The circulation of ascending money at 'big men's' feasts honours them, but obliges them, at the same time, to accept a more accurate evaluation of the real state of things. The efforts they make to elevate themselves, for a day, to the dignity of an ancestor have the unexpected result of reinforcing their submission to the general system of exchanges, which lures them into a display of their glory only better to encompass them.

What is more, the destruction of a 'big man's' coconut palms and gardens and the mockery and mimicry to which he is subjected, which are the principal themes of the feast, lead us to divine the presence, throughout the ceremony, of the ancestors themselves. Only after a 'big man's' feast may a garden be destroyed or the head of a coconut palm cut off without immediately provoking a violent reaction from the owner. We may well ask whether the men of the Panpipe groups who thus put the 'big man'

---

19. Generally a mountain whose inhabitants, under the aegis of a peace-master, have succeeded in establishing a zone where internal peace reigns.

in his place, exposing to ridicule his attempts to approach during his lifetime the fundamental value of an ancestor, do not, on this feast day, represent the ancestors themselves. At least two elements seem to support this conclusion.

A 'big man's' feast is musical, and only men associated with a Panpipe ensemble may attend. Music is always considered to be inspired by the ancestors' hidden presence, but at a 'big man's' feast, furthermore, certain specific musical themes are always played, each consisting of a single phrase without beginning or end which is unflaggingly repeated. The repetition of these phrases *ad infinitum* has the same rhythm as the 'linked successions' of a series of funeral feasts, of murders or of 'big men's' feasts, in which each dead person, murder victim or 'big man' 'covers' a previous one. This repetitive cadence is the very rhythm of the ancestors, contrasting sharply with the cadence of the exchanges carried out when killers and peace-masters confront one another (de Coppet and Zemp 1978: 126).

What is more, each compact group of men, musicians and dancers, carrying tall leafy branches, conceals in its midst its bundle of money, 'the child of the bamboo (music)' – that is, the image of a stillborn fetus – which it must carry to the foot of the platform. The men may not under any circumstances, on risk of death, so much as glance at this bundle, the sad fruit of their sterile ceremonial flirtations. In this regard as well they behave like ancestors, who abhor the blood of childbirth and the placenta.

There is thus ample reason to see in these men the ancestors, who occupy the stage at the feast and, in their mocking dance, give new impetus to the images of murder victims whom everyone would prefer to forget, since they recall the confrontations between killers and peace-masters. The ancestors thus intervene surreptitiously, at the precise moment that the 'big man' seemed to equal them, to impose their presence and remind the participants that they alone ratify all relations among the living and especially big men's socio-cosmic duties.

In conclusion to this brief analysis of the movements of ascending money (Sections 1 and 2), we should insist that while these prestations link tightly together certain persons and contribute to the cohesion of the groups constituted for these feasts, their primordial task is to perpetuate the circulation of images – ancestor-images at funeral feasts and murder victims' images at 'big men's' feasts. Ancestor-images are the society's supreme value, while murder victims' images are presented in a sort of parade of the men of the Panpipe groups around the ephemeral renown of a 'big man', himself at the service of this supreme value. Indeed, the great, inescapable task of all men and women, to which 'big men' consecrate themselves to an even higher degree than others, is the circulation of ancestor-images. Although each offering assumes the form of a personal act, and though this circulation constitutes the only locus where each member of society can accumulate monetary credits in complete security, personal interests do not predominate here. They are on the contrary completely subordinated to the law of the 'whole', of society and universe together. There is no higher authority than the circulation of ancestor-images. In the form of money, the value 'ancestor' is made tangible and may be offered again and again in movements which rule over all things and beings and, in particular, over men.

These exchanges, which perpetuate the society's fundamental value, intertwine with others, involving different kinds of prestations, which take the form of encounters, renewed from feast to feast, between two ceremonial groups ranged behind two 'big men', each the bearer of one of two opposing values. Such exchanges may be observed when blood money is paid, as well as at funeral feasts and at marriages. Blood money constitutes a third sort of purely monetary prestation, while at funeral feasts and marriages prestations of pigs and taros as well as money are offered.

The monetary prestation of the 'killer's' feast

This prestation is called the 'nine' (9), and consists of a large sum of money. Whoever avenges a true murder victim, by killing his murderer or someone close to him, a few weeks later receives a 'nine' equal to the bounty previously offered for a new victim. A 'nine' must also be paid to a killer who, after committing a murder, comes to an agreement with his victim's relatives to bring them in exchange the body of one of his own relatives who has violated some taboo. In either case, the preceding victim in the series is 'covered' by the new one, and this 'linked succession' appeases the former's breath.

During the feast for the payment of blood money, two 'big men', each accompanied by his nearest kinsmen and associates, confront one another: the killer, author of the latest murder, and the peace-master who benefits from the body the killer has provided. A low platform is erected within a wooden enclosure in the peace-master's village. Access to it is had by a short inclined plane whose last slat clacks each time someone treads on it. The killer sits on a bench at the further end of the platform as the men associated with the peace-master walk one by one up the inclined plane. Each of them makes the last slat resound with a sharp clack as he steps onto the platform. Then, striding back and forth, brandishing his spear, clacking the slat again and again, each recites the full series of his funeral sites and, finally, offers the killer his contribution toward the 'nine'.[20] The last person to mount onto the platform, clacking the slat, is the peace-master himself, whose offering completes the sum. In response, the killer then bounds forward, brandishing his spear, and recites the series of his murderous exploits. In his left hand he holds a mother-of-pearl incrusted ceremonial baton, and on his back he carries a bag called 'all in blossom', an example of the finest basketwork. The bag is adorned with a rattan chain, each of whose ring-shaped links represent one of his victims. In his hair he wears a cockade made of dolphin teeth. Striding back and forth, like the men who preceded him, he also punctuates his account with the clacking of the wooden slat.

A 'nine' is thus payment for a murder committed either by a killer unconnected to the prior victim's relatives and tempted by the bounty they have offered, or by the prior victim's killer against a member of his own entourage. In either event, it represents an additional sum, over and above an equalisation of losses – one death on each side – which is paid, in the first case, to a third party and, in the second, to the initial murderer. It increases the killer's monetary wealth, while at the same time confirming the prestige of the person who offers it as a peace-master, since he has not deviated from his pacific attitude despite the attack he has suffered and the loss of his relative. By offering a bounty or by indicating that he will accept a body from his aggressor, he commits himself to paying a large sum of money, thus adhering firmly to his style as peace-master. In so doing, he manages either to displace the conflict (since the first killer, after suffering the loss of a victim in return, will not turn against the peace-master, but rather against

20. The recitation by each man of his funeral sites stresses the relative nature of the peace-master's authority and also recalls that, in a murder settlement as well, the ancestors remain omnipotent.

the second killer who received the 'nine'), or to put an end to it (since his acceptance of a body offered by his aggressor and his payment of the 'nine' re-establish peace).

In either event, the 'nine' effects a 'stop' between the two groups initially involved in the confrontation. In the first case, however, the 'stop' is limited to the first killer's group and his victim's, while the affair continues between the first and second killers' groups. In the second, the 'stop' is definitive and, thereafter, the initial two groups can organise marriages and funeral feasts together, both of which, as we shall see below, continue the exchange relationship in another form.

Killers and peace-masters thus have diametrically opposed styles, with predictably different consequences. Killers quickly find themselves isolated, since no one wishes to risk becoming a substitute corpse. Peace-masters, on the contrary, who refuse to resort to murder and may even succeed in exporting it far from their 'territorial canoe', attract a growing number of people around them. Each time a 'nine' is paid, the difference between their situations is accentuated. The killer lives increasingly alone, must move constantly from place to place, and cannot tend a garden or raise pigs. The peace-master constantly enlarges the untroubled area around him, where work and feasts assume substantial proportions. Each region is divided between these two contrasting ways of life. The tranquil zones around peace-masters are fragile, however, since they are constantly menaced by killers' murderous attacks, and peace-masters must frequently pay out substantial sums in 'nines'. For their part, killers sometimes manage to change style by using their money to pay 'nines' and keep murder away, thereby themselves becoming peace-masters. The entirety of 'Are'are territory is divided between these two forms of social life, each of which predominates first in one part, then in another. The two are, however, intimately interrelated and depend on one and the same structure, that of 'Are'are exchanges.

From the socio-cosmic standpoint, where society and universe are one, a promise to pay a 'nine' enables a peace-master to obtain the breath of a new victim to 'cover' in 'linked succession' the breath of the previous one. The payment of a 'nine' is the only way to remove the menace of epidemic which hangs over a victim's entire family as long as his breath remains 'uncovered'. The possibility of acquiring a new victim's breath in return for a large sum of money demonstrates the enormous power of this money constituted of ancestor-images. It is so mighty that it can here impose a 'stop' in a series of murders. The ancestor-money of the 'nine' is the only means men dispose of to prevent a runaway chain of murders in which the breath of a new victim would always be required to 'cover' that of the preceding one. Money as a value thus encompasses the domain of murders in series. The styles of peace-master and killer are sharply defined and distinguished. The former pays out money to obtain his ancestors' gratitude for a 'covered' breath, while at the same time expelling subsequent murders from his sphere of influence, and sometimes even managing to put a stop to a series altogether. The latter procures a breath for the peace-master and collects the price of this service in money. If he was foreign to the affair in question, the price he receives is also a payment for his audacity, since by his act he calls down on his own head the vengeance of the previous killer.

We can now better understand how these two figures represent opposed, hierarchically related values. A peace-master, when he offers the ancestor-money of the 'nine', increases his 'territorial canoe's' prosperity in perfect harmony with the ancestors; he is on the side of life. A killer, in his breathless quest for one 'nine' after another, leaves a string of bodies behind him. He remains, however, caught up in the broader system. Fascinated by the peace-masters, he attacks them incessantly only better some day to equal them. A killer is, for the moment, on the side of murder, and each of his attacks deprives the ancestors of their right to decide on the moment of their descendant's death. From the perspective of the value system, the killer takes as his model the ancestors' murderous aspect, while the peace-master strives to represent the beneficent, regenerative aspects of the same ancestor-value. In the ceremony for the payment of the 'nine', the peace-master's value encompasses the killer's, although both 'big men' are indissolubly bound together in their mutual dependence on the supreme ancestor-value.

Thus far we have presented certain aspects of the circulation of money which demonstrate the identity of money with the ancestor-value, that is, with ancestor-images, and we have seen that this circulation gives meaning to the relations between persons and groups. We may now consider the other types of offerings, pigs and taros, which, together with monetary prestations, make up the complete system of prestations.

Further, while the fundamental superior value of image, of

which ancestors and money alike are constituted, is clear, we may raise the question of the respective values of breath and body. We now turn to an analysis of the prestations of pigs and taros, as well as other monetary prestations, at funeral feasts and then at marriage ceremonies.

The pigs, taros, and two associated monetary prestations of the funeral feast

Each of the two 'sides' of the feast, called 'the roots of the feast' (organised around the deceased's family) and 'the work of mourning' (organised around the grave-digger), must contribute an equal number of pigs and taros. The pigs are slaughtered and cut into pieces, the hunks of meat are cooked in an oven of hot stones, and the cooked meat is temporarily left on a stand. Each side constructs on the ground a large conical pile of taros and other vegetable foodstuffs, and places some of the pieces of cooked pork on top of it. These piles are exchanged between them, and then distributed to the guests, grouped by the villages from which they come. The meat and tubers are finally cut up and redistributed in small pieces to individuals, each of whom is free to decide whether he will make a meal of his share on the spot or return home to eat it.

Two monetary prestations are associated with the offerings of taros and pigs, one called 'stop-taros' and the other 'stop-quarrels'. The former is composed of short strands of money offered by various persons to the deceased's family, which receives them while standing on the platform. The latter, which closes the feast, consists of a large sum of money offered from the platform by the deceased's family to the grave-digger standing at its foot. There is no obligation to return either of these two prestations, which are thus given for good.

Nonetheless, if interpersonal relations alone are considered, the short strands of money of the 'stop-taros' may be seen as the repayment of small debts explicitly contracted with the deceased or certain of his relatives, or sometimes of implicit loans. From this standpoint, the 'stop-quarrels' may, in a similar fashion, be seen as a sum paid to the grave-digger to reimburse him for the pigs and taros he has contributed to the feast and to compensate him for the ritual service he has performed for the deceased. In this sense, the 'stop-taros' and the 'stop-quarrels' both close exchanges between persons by the payment of debts, owed to the deceased's family in the first case, or owed by them to the grave-digger in the second. These two monetary prestations both constitute 'stops', but while the 'stop-quarrels' is definitive, the 'stop-taros' appears in certain cases discreetly to invite an optional, uncertain return prestation.

Of the two, only the 'stop-quarrels' involves both of the ceremonial groups which are jointly responsible for the success of the feast or, more precisely, for the deceased's successful accession to the status of an ancestor. Their goal will be achieved only if each offers half of the pigs and half of the taros to be consumed, since this twofold contribution is essential to an ancestor's completeness. It is significant in this regard that there is often a relationship of affinity between the two ceremonial groups. The constitution of an ancestor in his plenitude thus depends on the conjunction of two elements, which, even when no marriage relationship exists between the groups, strongly resembles one. The 'stop-quarrels' should be seen as a 'stop' which settles and concludes the contribution of half the food necessary for the constitution of an ancestor. The parallel with marriage is all the more convincing since, at the close of the marriage ceremony, a very similar monetary prestation intervenes, imposing a 'stop' and settling the contribution of half the food consumed at the feast. And if, as is often the case, the grave-digger's and the deceased's families are indeed related by marriage, we may well raise the question whether there is not a 'linked succession' of some sort between the exchanges carried out at marriages and those at funeral feasts.

Before dealing with this problem, however, we should consider whether these prestations of pigs and taros and their conversion into money do not, like the previous prestations studied, have a meaning which transcends the spheres of interpersonal and inter-group relations. We have already seen that ancestor-images circulate in the unending round of ascending money at funeral feasts (Section 1); that murder victims' images reappear at 'big men's' feasts (Section 2); that murder victims' breaths must be 'covered' (Section 3); and that their bodies are displayed on the taro stand at 'big men's' feasts (Section 2). What happens, though, to those who die of illness, that is, whom their own ancestors condemn? Their images appear in their entirety at their funeral feasts, in the form of money suspended from the pole above the platform, but what is the fate of their breaths and their bodies?

The reconstitution of the dead person at his funeral feast is completed through the twofold contribution of pigs and taros, the former corresponding to breath and the latter to body. The three constituent elements of the 'Are'are universe are unequally distributed among the different beings. Cultivated plants are generally considered to have only body; domesticated pigs, body and breath; and humans, body, breath and image. Though a murder victim's breath must be 'covered' by another's, the breath of a person who succumbs to illness is 'covered' by the breaths of the pigs slaughtered and eaten at his funeral feast, while his body is 'covered' by the taros and other vegetable foodstuffs offered and consumed there. The deceased is thus decomposed into the three elements which in conjunction constituted him as a living human being. His image appears separately in all its monetary glory, suspended from the pole raised over the platform. In this way, it is propelled to the rank of ancestor and will bear the living person's name until the day he is completely forgotten. Humans, the sole possessors of image, alone partake of the encompassing value of the universe, associated with the ancestors, while body and breath are found as well in other living beings.

The twofold task of covering the deceased's body and breath devolves equally upon his family and upon the persons grouped around the grave-digger. Nonetheless, the contributions of taros and pigs at the feast have a particular relation to the two monetary prestations 'stop-taros' and 'stop-quarrels'.

As its name indicates, the 'stop-taros' ratifies and officially puts an end to the contribution of taros to the feast. Although half the taros are provided by the grave-digger, this monetary prestation, the sum of numerous individual contributions, is offered exclusively to the deceased's family, as if the presentation of the deceased's body in the form of taros were exclusively in the province of his family rather than in the grave-digger's. The essential point, however, is that the taros for the feast must be converted into money, owed to the deceased's family by individual debtors, and that this money operates a 'stop'. These interpersonal debts are all settled simultaneously on the occasion of the necessary transformation of the deceased's body into taros and of the taros into money. A person's funeral feast thus prompts the settlement in a single day of all the outstanding debts owed to each of his relatives, assuring thereby the ritual transformation:

> deceased's body ♦ taros eaten ♦ and finally 'stopped' in
> the form of money.

On the other hand, the 'stop-quarrels', which ratifies the contribution of the pigs' breaths, is offered exclusively by the deceased's family to the grave-digger's side, even though the pigs, like the taros, are provided in equal quantities by each of the two sides of the feast. It is as if the 'stop-quarrels' ratifies the 'linked succession' between the deceased's breath and the breaths of the pigs slaughtered at the feast, and concludes with the conversion of breath into money, all of which gives the ritual transformation:

> deceased's breath ♦ pigs eaten ♦ and finally 'stopped' in
> the form of money.

The 'stop-quarrels' received by the grave-digger when a person dies of illness corresponds to the 'nine' received by a killer where a murder victim is concerned. Both prestations ratify the contribution of the breath essential for the decisive ritual task of 'covering' each dead person's breath by another. In the case of a murder victim, of course, the breath provided is always of human origin, while in that of someone who dies of illness it is furnished by the slaughter of domesticated pigs. This distinction indicates not only that the paths followed by a murder victim's breath and the breath of someone who dies of illness are different, but also that pigs, through their breath, play a role which is doubtless determinative in the recycling and renewal of men's breath beyond death.

On analysis, the entire funeral feast thus seems to be a sequence of operations aimed at separating the three constituent elements – image, breath and body – which were united in the living person and are present, respectively, in the form of the three 'species' (like of the Eucharist) – money, pigs and taros. The conversion of the deceased's image into ancestor-money is the ceremony's most important result. This transformation is indispensable if the dead person is to be elevated to the dignity of ancestor and new impetus given to the circulation of ancestor-money, which orders all the other exchanges and tirelessly bears witness to the fundamental relation between men and ancestors. The transformations of breath into pigs and of body into taros are subordinated to this circulation and are both closed by monetary prestations, respectively the 'stop-quarrels' and the 'stop-taros'. Thus all three of the deceased's constituents have been publicly displayed in monetary form in the movements of shell-money to and from the ceremonial platform. The image takes the form of the strands of shell-money attached to the pole raised above the platform, the money representing the breath is handed down from the platform and given to the grave-digger standing at its foot, and that representing the body is handed up to the deceased's family standing on the platform. Since the platform's structure transposes the different levels of the universe – its floor represents the surface of the earth, where gardens are planted, and the surface of the sea, while its overhanging pole figures everything above and its substructure everything beneath (de Coppet 1976),[21] it is clear that at the end of the funeral feast the three monetary substitutes for the three constituent elements occupy abnormal and exceptionally lethal positions. The monetary image has left the surface where ordinary affairs and life itself have their place and has ascended to ancestral life. The money which 'stops' the pigs appears to be buried in the ground, though breath can normally only be imagined on the surface of the earth. And the money which 'stops' the taros seems to be uprooted and placed on the ground, where tubers rot. These three sums are thus completely out of place with respect to the things they represent, which have nonetheless been entirely converted into money and thereby 'stopped'.[22] But if funeral feasts, after separating and differentiating what the living person united, finally resolve everything into money, what do marriage feasts do?

The pigs, taros, and associated monetary prestations of the marriage feast

When a marriage is to be celebrated, the bride is first led to her future husband's dwelling, where she lives for a certain time. A

21. The article cited discusses the projection of the platform's three levels onto the cosmic plane in three Solomon Island societies.

22. If this disposition of money is taken as an illustration of part of the 'Are'are system of classification, it would show that this system stresses movements rather than fixed, material locations, since the relations between the different elements have more importance than the elements considered individually, and can only be understood in the context of a hierarchy which may be inverted by imperatives arising from the general circulation.

feast is then organised in her parents' village. The 'man's side'[23] offers her parents a large sum of money, which is suspended from a horizontal pole supported at each end by a post about six feet high, and the amount of money thus displayed is publicly proclaimed. The larger it is, the more prestigious the marriage, the greater the respect and pride with which the wife is considered by her own relatives and her husband's, and the more onerous and dangerous it will be to interfere with the integrity of the union, especially by adultery.

Nonetheless, although this large sum of money is displayed in its entirety on the pole, it is not offered to the 'woman's side' in one lot. Rather, one or more 'heads of money', *pau na pata*,[24] are presented by each member of the man's side to one or several members of the woman's side. These 'heads' may be offered in four different ways. A small part of the total sum is offered for good, since it is not matched by any later, obligatory return prestation. This fraction is called 'to stop the woman', that is, to marry and have children with her; henceforth, she belongs to her husband's family. The other three parts are offered subject to a later obligation to give something in return for them, either an equivalent amount of money, or live pigs, or taros to replant. These monetary loans fall due on the day of the return marriage feast *torana*.

This second feast takes place two or three years later and is held in the husband's parents' village. The wife's relatives bring with them a large number of pigs and taros. When they arrive, they first pay back the part of the sum lent to them, which must be returned in money. Then they offer the live pigs and the taros to replant to the persons who had given them the parts of the initial loan which were to be repaid in that form. Thereafter, both the wife's and the husband's sides offer pigs and taros, which are consumed at a large meal. Finally, the husband's side offers two distinct sums of money to the wife's, one for the taros and the other for the pigs that they contributed to the meal. These two monetary prestations close the return feast.

23. In place of the usual terms 'wife-givers' and 'wife-takers', which generally refer to transgenerational systems of marriage-alliance, we have adopted here the 'Are'are expressions 'woman's side' for those who give a woman in marriage and 'man's side' for those who receive her. Indeed, among the 'Are'are, another marriage between the same two groups may not be celebrated during the same or the following three generations. Only in the fourth generation may cousins marry. The expressions 'woman's side' and 'man's side' reflect, furthermore, that the two sides cannot reverse positions – there is no sister exchange.

24. A 'head' is a large unit of money, composed of one or more fathom-long strands of shell-beads.

Chart 2 summarises the various exchanges observed in the course of the two marriage feasts.

Analysis of these exchanges is facilitated by the fact that each of them manifests procedures already observed in other exchanges. Viewed in this light, marriage would seem to be a combination of relations specific to other domains.

The money to 'stop the woman', first of all, although only a small part of the total sum attached to the pole, may be interpreted as a sort of payment to the woman's side for having furnished a wife for the man's side. This monetary prestation is similar to the 'nine', since it is also definitive (that is, not returned), is accompanied by the same gesture of brandishing a spear, and recognises the signal service rendered to the husband's family by the providing of a wife, just as the 'nine' acknowledges the providing of the new victim required by a prior murder victim's family. The analogy is even more eloquent in the case where a killer's victim is a member of his own group. We can thus safely affirm that giving away a wife is formally similar for her family to her social murder, since henceforth she belongs principally to her husband's family. This monetary prestation 'stops the woman' for her family of origin; more precisely, it 'stops' her image, the part of her person which signifies the totality of a human being.

The other three sorts of prestations which go to make up the money suspended from the pole are also offered to the woman's side, but are of a completely different nature, since the sums involved are only lent and must be paid back two or three years later at the return feast. The only monetary loans we have encountered thus far are those represented by the 'ascending money' at funeral feasts (Section II) and at 'big men's' feasts (Section II). At the former, the image of a person who has died of illness is constituted in this way, while, at the latter, murder victims' images put in an anonymous appearance. In the marriage ceremony, however, the money lent by the man's side to the woman's side is not returned completely in monetary form, but in the form of all three 'species', money, pigs and taros.

The marriage feast thus accomplishes a series of ritual transformations which are the inverse of those carried out at the funeral feast. In the marriage ceremony, money alone is ritually converted into the three 'species', taros to replant (bearers of body), live pigs to raise (bearers of breath) and, finally, money itself (entirely image). The marriage feast seems capable of re-creating the living

Chart 2

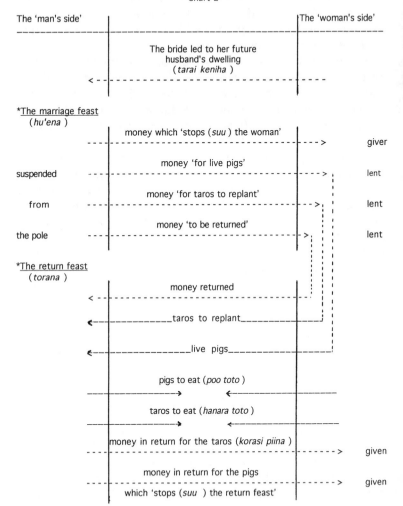

forms of body and breath, tangibly represented by the taros and pigs offered to the man's side, from ancestor-money constituted exclusively of image. And just as the grave-digger at a funeral feast is responsible for safeguarding the deceased's image, which he must return in full at the return funeral feast, here the woman's side bears full responsibility for the repayment of the money offered by the man's side, but also, and above all, for its conversion into the three fundamental elements. The ritual task of the woman's side is to re-create body, breath and image from money, which at the end of the funeral feast had subsumed the three in image. The grave-digger and the woman's side thus both have an extremely intimate relationship with the ancestors, since they are the privileged agents, respectively, of the separation of human life into its three elements or 'species' which are then converted into money, and of the reconversion of money into the same three 'species', differentiated and alive, ready to reunite in newborn children. Further, when, as frequently occurs, the grave-digger is also the deceased's affine, he is always chosen from the 'man's side', which, in this case, is charged with the transformation of its dead affine into an ancestor and into money. Since the woman's side is always responsible for converting the money received from the man's side into the three 'living' 'species', affinity relations often bear the heavy burden of both these opposite ritual tasks, which are alike submitted to the authority of the ancestor-money.

Marriage feasts are characterised by this anticipation of the life-giving synthesis of the three fundamental elements, and thus seem to be a sort of funeral in reverse. Indeed, starting with ancestor-money, a marriage prepares the way for future births, while a funeral feast, starting with a dead person, soon separated into his three constituent elements, converts them all into money. From a Western, individualistic standpoint, marriages are seen as taking place during life and funerals after it. From the holistic 'Are'are standpoint, all things are seen as encompassed in a circulation which is the foundation of the universe, and the supreme task of both marriages and funerals is situated beyond death and before life. Both ceremonies are links in a chain which connects death caused by the ancestors to the synthesis of what is human in conception and birth. The woman's side takes in charge the second of these two 'linked successions', which together permit the constant renewal of life, after an obligatory passage through an exclusively monetary, ancestral stage. Money is thus simultaneously the op-

erative factor and the tangible locus of these two opposite meta-
morphoses.

It only remains to examine the conclusion of the return marriage
feast, where both the prestations offered and the meal which follows recall the funeral feast. From the socio-cosmic standpoint, the
two sides of the feast, each of which contributes the same quantities of pigs and taros, reconstitute and then make a meal of the
wife's breath and body. But, it may be objected, the wife is not dead!
She was married just two years before and is alive and well. All
that is true enough for her husband's family; but not for her family of origin, which has lost all its rights over her. The prestations
offered at the end of the return marriage feast, by metaphorically
reconstituting the wife's body and breath, constitute for her relatives a sort of mourning ceremony, and her family, like the deceased's at a funeral, provides half the pigs and taros required for
a mourning repast.

From the standpoint of the ceremonial groups, however, the
woman's side, which receives from the man's side the two monetary prestations called 'in return for the taros' and 'in return for
the pigs' brought to be eaten at the feast, is in a position compara-
ble to that of the grave-digger at a funeral feast, who receives the
'stop-quarrels' in return for the prestations he has contributed and
for his aid in transforming the deceased into an ancestor. At the
conclusion of the marriage ceremony, the woman's side receives
these two sums of money in return for its contributions of pigs and
taros, and for its aid in transferring the bride's body and breath to
the 'man's side'. For the wife's family of origin, the two monetary
prestations 'stop' her body and breath by converting them into
money. From their standpoint, her marriage is the funeral of her
body and breath, while for the husband's family it is – not the
advent of a new ancestor, but – the confirmation that the bride's
body and breath belong henceforth to them.

The two marriage feasts taken together seem to borrow several
sequences from funeral ceremonies, for example, the money displayed on the pole which is lent to the woman's side for two years,
and the contributions made by each side of equal quantities of pigs
and taros to be eaten before being converted into money. Indeed,
the woman's side accomplishes ritual work which is the opposite
of the grave-digger's, by converting money, entirely image, into
the three 'species', ready for synthesis in future births. The woman's side, at the same time, also carries out the work of mourning

for the wife's body and breath.

What is the relative significance of affinity and consanguinity in these two ceremonies, and how are they related? We have noted the woman's side's importance in the ritual work of marriage, and have seen that the grave-digger is often chosen by the deceased's family from among those who have married his sisters, that is, from his sisters' husbands' families. These factors would tend to lend importance to affinity; which is, however, of only fleeting significance, since a person's affines become his children's blood relations. From this viewpoint, the ritual work both of marriages and funerals (if the grave-digger is chosen among the deceased's sisters' husbands) consists in bringing together the same two ceremonial moieties and fusing them in a common product, be it 'children' or an ancestor. Once a marriage has been performed, affinity loses importance to bilateral consanguinity, that is, to a relationship with common ancestors. The bipolarity of affinity gives way to the compact mass of consanguinity, in conformity with and submission to the ancestor-value and the movements of ancestor-money.

*

Our study of the movement of the different sorts of prestations in the various 'Are'are ceremonies reveals two sharply differentiated levels of value:

(a) On the superior level, funerals and marriages perform the ritual work vital to the renewal of society and of the universe in their three fundamental elements, image, breath and body. The most vital part of this task is the transformation of the dead into their three constituent elements, which are then all converted into money. Marriage performs the inverse operation by transforming money into the three distinct elements, foreshadowing their possible reunion in newborn children. Of the three fundamental elements, image has the highest value and represents the whole. Humanity participates in this whole through each person's image, which, after death and before birth, is entirely transformed into shell-money, the anonymous material embodiment of the ancestors.

The transformation of the living into ancestors, into image-money, is 'Are'are society's great task. Money is not here simply a universal equivalent; it 'is' the ancestors. Its circulation establishes the contours of the whole, of society and universe understood as one. That this whole must be ceaselessly churned up by exchanges and converted into ancestor-money, only serves to lend it a perfect, immutable coherence. 'Image' in its cyclical round encompasses the living, whose activities are dominated by their obligation to assure the perpetuation of this endless, constantly renewed circulation. Image governs as well the circulation of breath and body and of their avatars, pigs and taros, which are also transformed, again and again, into money.

Image is everywhere. It is each person's essential part and his whole, as well as the promise of his inevitable dissolution in the whole. It is omnipresent in the society's exchanges, in the obligatory conversion of what is exchanged into image-money which must circulate unceasingly, so dangerous is it, constant threat of death, unfailing promise of life. Image is the ancestors, one's own and all the others, and all the customs which must be reassumed, re-enacted and nourished by men's efforts in taro gardens conquered from the forest, with pigs patiently domesticated in the forest, in the making of ornaments and in the fabrication of fathom-long strands of money from shell-beads ceaselessly strung on new twisted fibres. Image is, finally, what alone remains of all the forgotten ancestors who have departed for the Island Lost-Forevermore but who remain present in the society's incorruptible shell-money.

Chart 3 summarises all the various transformations, and presents graphically the society as a whole, pervaded and circumscribed by the ancestor-money, caught up in its whirling circulation. The movement of the whole is represented by the outer, encompassing circuit. If we choose to start, arbitrarily, from the living and persons who have died of illness, this loop traverses funerals, attains its peak at ancestor-money, traverses marriages and returns once again to births and the living. It encloses another circuit whose activities seem the exclusive affair of the living and concern the vain fate of murder victims. In this inner, encompassed circuit, peace masters and killers give and receive the money which confines them all in a common submission to the ancestors. Finally, although the question is not treated in the text, we have included here the transformations undergone by the corpses of the two sorts of dead to indicate their return to the state of taros and pigs. (For a discussion of this question, see de Coppet 1981.)

CHART 3

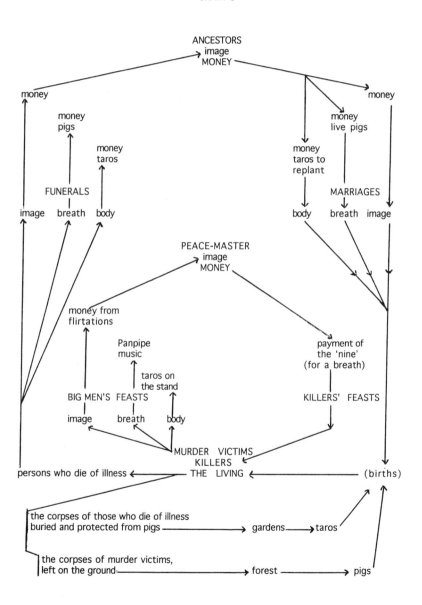

(b) Encompassed within this whole, the inferior level is, strictly speaking, that of the living, where peace-masters and killers accomplish their inseparable tasks. These two sorts of 'big men' incarnate contrasting values. The peace-master is associated with the ancestors in general and, in particular, with the intermediate ancestors, those who have been transformed into money, that is, with the system's ultimate, encompassing value. The killer, on the contrary, is associated with the subordinated value of individual action which obeys a code of provocation. He has no connection either with the intermediate ancestors or with money, the ultimate value, and is associated rather with his agnatic apical ancestor. The latter is at the origin of generations of male descendants and marks the place of their first local settlement. The killer thus signifies a point of departure, the absence of money, the oneness and immobility of origins. This value is epitomised by him among the living, but is subordinated to the intermediate ancestors who have acceded to ancestral life through the money of funeral feasts.

The intermediate ancestors remain outside the domain which yawns open each time a killer supplants them by administering death in their place. The fate of murder victims is quite remarkable. Denied the last rites which would make ancestors of them, they are given a sort of mock funeral at 'big men's' feasts. Their constituent elements – body, breath and image – do not disappear, but are placed at the service of the renown of 'big men' whose image they help to construct.

Nonetheless, the ancestors' surreptitious presence, in the person of the men of the Panpipe groups, reaffirms the domination of money and the ancestors over both the 'big man's' glory and the murder victims' endlessly gyrating course. Indeed, the overall movement results from a tension between the ultimate value, the intermediate ancestors and money, associated with the peace-masters, and the opposing value of individual initiative, represented by the killers, in exclusive relation with their apical ancestors. In each ritual, the two figures of peace-master (dominant) and killer (subordinated) oppose one another. The former is on the side of life, the latter on the side of untimely death, which expels murder victims out of the encompassing circuit and leaves them on the fringes of society.

Thus the supreme value, represented by the intermediate ancestors and by the money which is consubstantial with them, rules and at the same time constructs and composes the whole, while at a lower level the peace-master, in opposition to the killer, constantly re-establishes the supremacy of this same value.

It should now be clearer how sterile it would have been, in studying a society which projects itself into the universe and considers itself responsible for life's constant renewal, to have adopted either the point of view of the Western individual 'subject', unjustifiably imposed on the so-called partners to 'Are'are exchanges, or that of the supposed 'objects of exchange', tracked down and forced into the straitjacket of presumed empirical reciprocity. Every activity of 'Are'are society forms part of an ensemble, of an immense ritual project whose operations succeed one another in a necessary order. There are, first of all, the different series of identical 'linked successions', of which sequential murders, each essential to 'cover' the breath of the preceding victim, are the most striking example. These series may be compared to the *piling up* of similar actions in a locus which is neither that of the partners to the exchanges nor of the quantified objects of exchange, but rather the social locus *par excellence*, where 'Are'are society repeats the ritual work necessary to the endless pursuit of harmony with its universel. In this same social locus, the various *transformations* also succeed one another. Going beyond a simple piling up, they constantly usher the three fundamental elements through life into death and through death into life, expressing in this way the force of the supreme value, the ancestors. These transformations connect operations as diverse as the giving of death by the ancestors or by the living, ingestion, gardening and pig-raising, as well as ceremonial offerings on the platform and the 'stops' marked by conversions into money. All these *linked transformations* contribute, in a precise and immutable order, to the constant renewal of a whole which, in its movement, is and becomes 'Are'are society.

III: Tanebar-Evav

A study of exchanges at Tanebar-Evav is one of the best ways of achieving an overview of the society. Since the exchanges carried out in relation with marriage are the most characteristic, we begin by examining them in some detail. In a second section, we extend our analysis to the ceremonies which direct the annual ritual millet cultivation cycle and then suggest how the society may be understood as a totality, in terms of its fundamental values.

Marriage exchanges

At Tanebar-Evav, the exchanges associated with asymmetric marriage do not, at first sight, seem to involve the participation of the entire society. Two exchange groups, *yan ur* and *mang oho*, centred respectively around the 'houses' of the groom and the bride, organise a new marriage within a pre-existing inter-marriage relationship or inaugurate a new such relationship. These groups exchange prestations intended both for the living and for supernatural beings. Of particular interest are the offerings made to the *duad-nit*, who include certain living persons and certain of the dead, all in association with the god. The term *duad-nit* designates, in a general way, the 'wife-givers' and their ancestors, that is, both the bride's and the groom's maternal uncles, as well as the members of all the houses which at one time or another have occupied the position of 'wife-giver' for either of the two central houses. It means literally the 'god' (*duad*) – the 'dead' (*nit*). (The word *nit* is also used to designate a corpse.) *Nit* should be taken here, however, in a very broad sense. Indeed, to name the *nit* the villagers often associate two adjectives *mamatan-vavan*, 'dead–living', incorporating in the same category both the dead of the 'wife-givers' house and the 'wife-givers' themselves. A similar expression, *itaten mamatan-vavan*, 'the dead and living elders', is used in the same fashion to refer to those who exercise authority in the village.

The marriage relationship is called *yan ur – mang oho*, 'children-sister – people of the village', an expression whose two terms designate respectively the bridegroom's group and the bride's group. The latter is considered superior to the former and, as its name 'people of the village' indicates, is conceived of as being from the village itself, while the 'children-sister' group is, in consequence, implicitly considered as originating elsewhere.[25] The marriage relationship is thus envisaged from the standpoint of the 'people of the village', who are associated with a particular locality. If we consider that the origin of houses was connected with the first gift of a woman in marriage, that the category 'people of the

25. Even though Tanebar-Evav village is in fact almost completely endogamous.

village' is associated with belonging to a village, and that a reference to the dead implies one to the god, we may conclude that, at least in the context of intermarriage, the values associated with the 'people of the village' are those of *haratut*, the society considered from the viewpoint of its internal relations, in opposition to those of *lór*, the society open to the outside world.

Once created, a relationship *yan ur – mang oho* continues even if no further marriages are contracted between the two groups. This bond is indeed never simply limited to a single exchange of what we call a marriage compensation for a woman. It always involves an unceasing exchange of prestations, as well as other reciprocal duties and obligations, throughout the lives of persons involved, and thereafter binds the two houses to one another for ever. Each house or exchange unit is thus enmeshed in a network of inter-marriage relationships whose origin is lost in the mists of time. For a house at one pole of such a relationship, the house at the other is exclusively either *yan ur* or *mang oho*, except in the very rare case of *sivelek* marriage, which involves the reciprocal exchange of women. In addition to this network, houses are also linked to each other by formalised relations of mutual assistance or of dependency.[26] Each time a house is directly involved in some important event, all the houses connected with it by relationships of one sort or another offer their support. The entire village is thus present at every exchange, with half of the houses grouped around each of the two principal actors. Each house participates, however, only by dint of the specific dual relationships uniting it to certain other houses. These exchanges between houses cannot thus be analysed in the same way as those which we consider below in which the society acts as a totality.

The work of marriage exchanges – the arranging of marriages, the organisation of marriage ceremonies, the transfers involved in the exchanges themselves, in short, everything involved in creat-ing or renewing a marriage relationship between two groups – is called *urat yab van*, 'the task of weaving a single piece of basketry'.

---

26. The mutual assistance relationship *baran ya'an war*, 'elder brother–younger brother', is created initially by an agreement between two men, and implies the equal status of the groups (generally houses) involved; either of the two may ask the other for assistance. The dependency relationship *ko-maduan*, 'little one–master', implies that the 'little one' is under an obligation to the master and must perform various services for him. (This latter relationship should not be confused with the noble–servant relationship – often called the noble–slave or noble–dependent relationship – which binds a noble's servants to his house.)

Urat also signifies the veins, the arteries and, here, a collective effort of mutual assistance whose result is the wife. The expression illustrates how the villagers conceive of the 'work' of these exchanges: circulation of the blood, which nourishes the relationship; intertwining of the fibres which are its woof and warp.

(a) The 'marriage compensation'
In an asymmetric marriage, the return prestation *ôt velin* offered by the *yan ur* is composed essentially of a cannon, gongs, pieces of jewellery of differing value, and sometimes of paper money and coins. These offerings are one way for the *yan ur* to honour the *duad-nit*. In this way, the *yan ur 'flurut duad-nit'*, that is, 'let the *duad-nit* gorge themselves'. All these prestations collectively bear the name *kubang-mas* 'money-gold', and they are all considered money. The cannon offered at the marriage ceremony is called *ngaban tenan*, 'the keel and first plank [of the sailing-boat]', and the gong is given the name *hibo ni leat vehe*, 'the poles and paddles of the sailing-boat'. The cannon is said to 'replace' the bride's body.

Certain sorts of goods also circulate from the *mang oho* to the *yan ur*: plates and cloth, household items and kitchen implements. Plots of land are also sometimes transferred to them. These prestations are grouped under the name *bingan-sibo*; 'plates–cloth', and the *mang oho* are said 'to feed–to clothe', *fa'an fnólók* the *yan ur* with them.

In every exchange between the parties to a marriage relationship, but also between those to relationships of mutual assistance or dependency, the monetary prestations of cannons, gongs and jewellery are called 'money-gold', and the prestations of plates and cloth 'plates–cloth'. However, only the 'money-gold' prestations offered by *yan ur* are called 'to let the *duad-nit* gorge themselves', while all other prestations, 'money-gold' and 'plates–cloth' alike, are termed 'to feed–to clothe'. In addition to 'money-gold', *yan ur*, like servants in their relations with nobles, must constantly offer their *mang oho* comestibles (a portion of the game they take or of their catch, palm wine and all sorts of other foodstuffs). *Mang oho*, on the contrary, never offer food to their *yan ur*, and one may well ask why their prestations are called 'to feed'. It is obviously not a question here of real foodstuffs, but rather of the possibility offered the *yan ur* who are 'fed' to multiply and prosper, since a woman given in marriage bears in herself a promise of life and progeny. The *yan ur*, for their part, let the *duad-nit* take for themselves 'food which does not feed', whose value depends not on the growth it produces but rather on the recognition it represents of the power of life and death vested in the *duad-nit*.

The prestations offered at the marriage ceremony itself cannot be correctly understood without integrating them in the ensemble of exchanges through which the continuing relationship between *mang oho* and *yan ur* manifests itself.[27]

When a child is born, for example, the men of a house go to sea to catch fish and hunt tortoises, which are then consumed by the old people of the village and by representatives of their *mang oho* at the child's naming ceremony *ót meman* ('to make the name'). It is said that the men went to seek the child's name in the sea. This prestation is again called *flurut duad-nit*. It is in virtue of this ceremony that the child becomes a member of the society, under the protection of the god, the dead and the *mang oho*.

When a *mang oho*'s house is rebuilt, one of his *yan ur* sometimes offers him a cannon, especially if the full marriage compensation was not given at a marriage ceremony some time before. This prestation is also called *flurut duad-nit*, but the cannon is now designated 'the ridge-pole [of the house]' and not 'the keel [of the sailing-boat]'. The *mang oho* offer cloth and plates in return. When an old man dies, a cannon offered by his children to his house's *mang oho* some time after his funeral is called *nit vokan*, 'the dead person's replacement'.

On each of these occasions the *yan ur*, in addition to foodstuffs, thus provide a cannon which, at a marriage, is said to replace the bride's body and, in other circumstances, is identified with something else closely related to the *mang oho*, the ridge-pole of their house or even the corpse of one of their descendants. In this last case, the corpse, which must eventually disappear, is replaced implicitly by the cannon, as if to assure the deceased's continued presence in another form. In exchange for the life (that is, the blood) furnished by the *mang oho*, the *yan ur* through their monetary prestations provide the *mang oho* with a ritual service which is just as indispensable. For each woman received in marriage, they offer a cannon which replaces a key element either of the *mang oho*'s sailing-boat or of their house. At the death of persons born from a marriage, the cannon returned to the *mang oho* replaces the life or

27. Although we translate *yan ur-mang oho* relationship by 'intermarriage' relationship, it should be quite clear however that this expression describes only partially this relationship which extends far beyond marriage itself.

blood itself which was given through the mother.

Two points should be stressed:

• First, the specificity of the *yan ur*'s relation with the *mang oho*, which, unlike any other sort of binary inter-house relationship at Tanebar-Evav, involves a relation with supernatural beings, the *duad-nit*.

In all the various types of relationships that exist between houses, one of the two parties occupies an inferior position: in the dependency relationship, for example, the 'little ones' with regard to their master, and in the marriage relationship, the *yan ur* with regard to the *mang oho*. However, although in all the various relationships prestations of the same kind (money, foodstuffs) are offered to the houses with superior status, the subordination does not have the same meaning in the marriage relationship, since it alone involves a direct tie to supernatural beings.

Further, the binary relationship binding a 'little one' to his master is immutable, and does not form part of a system in conjunction with other similar relationships. In contrast, the *yan ur*'s position with regard to their *mang oho* is in a certain sense relative, since in this system of asymmetric marriage they are themselves also *mang oho* in relation to those who take their women and with regard to whom they play the role of representatives of the *duad-nit*, that is, of their own ancestors.

The various exchange relationships can thus not be defined simply in terms of the kinds of prestations which are offered. The same goods, designated by the same expressions, 'money-gold' and 'plates–cloth', circulate in opposite directions between *yan ur* and *mang oho*, between masters and 'little ones', and between the houses in a mutual assistance relationship. The marriage relationship is exceptional, however, in that, in addition to the exchange of prestations, the taking of a woman in marriage also involves, in return, the establishment of a relationship with supernatural beings. Marriage here does not, therefore, consist simply of an exchange of a woman against certain goods.

• Second, the uniqueness of the exchanges between *mang oho* and *yan ur*, which involve the transmission of life itself.

Through the woman they give in marriage, the *mang oho* offer life to their *yan ur*, while at the same time threatening them with death. They are, in a way, responsible for the perpetuation and prosperity of the *yan ur*'s house. This is particularly clear in their obligation to come and consume their *yan ur*'s game, fish and tortoises after the birth of a child to the latter's house, ratifying in this way the social existence of the newborn infant who henceforth is endowed with a name recognised by the *duad-nit*.

What precisely is involved in *ôt velin*, 'the ritual work of return' in marriage? And what is the sense of the different names given to the cannon at the marriage ceremony, on the construction of a house, and at a funeral? While the entire marriage compensation is to be understood as a return prestation, a cannon offered at the marriage ceremony itself is specifically said 'to replace' the woman's body and is called the 'keel and first plank [of the sailing-boat]'. In contrast, a cannon offered on the occasion of the construction of the *mang oho*'s house is spoken of as the house's 'ridge-pole', while one given at a funeral is designated 'the replacement for the dead person' and replaces his corpse. In all three of these contexts, the *yan ur* contribute something which is essential for the *mang oho*: a sailing-boat's fundamental element, the ridge-pole which permits the roof to be put in place and a house to be sealed and, finally, money to replace a dead person's life. In the first two cases, it is a question of completing a container, an outer envelope, and in the last, of replacing a life given through a preceding marriage. A house, a sailing-boat, a human body are containers of life whose continued existence is assured by the *yan ur*'s prestations, while the contents – life, blood, everything that makes up men themselves – are in the hands of the *duad-nit*. The *mang oho*'s house would not be complete without the prestations of their *yan ur*, who, to replace a woman given in marriage, contribute a metaphorical 'ridge-pole' in the form of a cannon, which guarantees the house's tightness in inclement weather; similarly, a sailing-boat is above all its keel.

The very existence of a 'house' as a social and exchange unit is inextricably bound up with the close association all these exchanges create between *yan ur* and *mang oho*. A house is not simply defined by the existence of a lineage composed of the descendants of a single ancestor. Anthropological theory has accustomed us to reasoning in terms of exchange units, of lineages and groups which exchange women. Here, however, the perspective is reversed. The exchanges themselves create the units through the joint contributions of each house's *mang oho*, who furnish it with women and life, its content, and of its *yan ur*, who consolidate its outer envelope, its container. It might even be said that a house only exists as the consequence of the exchange relationship between the dead and the living, between the *duad-nit*, who give life and take it away, and the *yan ur*, who honour the dead and protect life by watching over its containers.

Tanebar-Evav society can thus not be accounted for adequately solely in terms of the exchange of women. Nor does the attempt to calculate some sort of empirical reciprocity really shed much light on marriage exchanges. Although in the 'ritual work of marriage' *ót velin*, as in all other exchanges, a gift of 'money-gold' is indeed always followed by a counter-gift 'to feed–to clothe', the two prestations should be viewed, together, as a 'return' *velin* in which the cannon 'replaces' the woman. The gift of the woman herself is, furthermore, never explicitly alluded to; only the return, her replacement by money, is mentioned. At most it can be said that there are here neither gains nor losses. In reality, the *mang oho* think of the gift they receive of a cannon and gongs as guaranteeing the continued existence of their house, just as they consider that the gift they offer of a woman ensures continued life for their *yan ur*.

The superiority of *mang oho* over *yan ur* is founded on the former's quality as representatives of the supernatural forces who are the guardians of life and death.

What of the subject–object distinction here? The status of what is exchanged seems indeed to fluctuate with the circumstances. A cannon replaces a woman's body in the same way that an adopted son replaces his adoptive father on the latter's death. But a cannon is also, on other occasions, compared to the keel of a sailing-boat, while a sailing-boat is itself sometimes likened to a house. And though a sailing-boat is at times considered an object of exchange, at other times it is conceived of as a body, *itumun*, which is itself to be replaced.

What is more, the place in the society's value system of precisely the same objects varies completely in accordance with the kind of relationship in which they are exchanged. In the case of marriage, the prestation consisting of a cannon and gongs is linked to the dead (*flurut duad-nit*); in the context of other relationships (mutual assistance, dependency), prestations composed of the same goods have no relation to the dead and are simply offered 'to feed–to clothe', *fa'an fnólók*. The nature of an exchange relationship is thus not tied to the *kinds* of 'objects' which circulate, whose movements alone never allow us to characterise an exchange. The relationship itself has precedence.

(b) The ceremonial prestations of the marriage ritual
Once a marriage has been decided upon, and after numerous preliminary meetings between the two houses directly interested as well as those assisting them, the ceremony itself takes place. It unfolds at several different houses, chosen because of their relationships with the bride's and bridegroom's houses.

In a ceremony performed before the entire village, the betrothed share a plate of rice, served in a conical pile with a hard-boiled egg on top. The egg symbolises the unity necessary if the marriage relationship is to endure.[28] A woman from the bride's house then hangs a sort of small, plaited basket around the bridegroom's neck. It contains, among other things, half a betel leaf, a little tobacco, one of two black stones (probably small meteorites, said to be the testicles of the rain or of the tornado which fell from the sky after an overly violent copulation with the clouds), and two small dry fruits found washed up on the beach, one of which is vulviform. Once the basket is in place, the groom may not speak to the woman who brought it to him until some days later, when, after bringing her an offering of game he has killed and fish he has caught, he returns the basket's contents to her. The offering he makes to her consists of the same sorts of things that *yan ur* continually offer their *mang oho*.

The marriage ritual also includes the killing of several pigs offered by the groom's group, together with a small amount of money, to the spirits *mitu* guardians of the bride's and the groom's houses.[29] This prestation, called *sisinga un – man bubur*, 'head of the conical rice cake – chicken gruel', is intended to advise them that the bride is leaving her house of birth and henceforth belongs to her husband's house. The pigs are later consumed by the guests at the meal which closes the marriage feast.

Several prestations are also offered to the dead. The bride's or the groom's group, or both, may sometimes present food and a

28. This ritual is also performed on other occasions when unity is to be affirmed, at an man's initiation as an elder, for example, or when a sailing-boat departs (or returns, and unity is restored).

29. The *mitu* are of two sorts: guardians of the village (there are five principal ones, each of whom protects a particular part of it), and guardians of houses. Most of the *mitu* are said to have come originally from off the island; certain are specifically Moslem; one is an ancestor.

small amount of money to one of three patrilineal ancestors said
to be present at three fixed points in the surrounding forest. This
category of the dead is also invoked to assure successful childbirth,
which in local sayings is described as a sort of departure from the
island. Each side also offers a prestation of palm wine, tobacco and
betel leaves to its own *duad-nit*, that is, to the god and to the dead
of the bride's and the bridegroom's maternal uncles.[30]

An analysis of these three aspects of the marriage ritual will permit us to achieve a better understanding of the society's fundamental values, *haratut* and *lór*.

Offerings to the *duad-nit* are the only occasion on which an individual or a house addresses the god directly, other than in collective ceremonies which involve the whole society conceived of
as *haratut*. The *mang oho* thus appear to be the unique human intermediaries between men and the god.[31] While prestations are
only offered to the dead of the forest on certain fixed occasions,
such as marriage and childbirth, the villagers make offerings to and
consult the *duad-nit* constantly, in every sort of circumstance
throughout their lives. The *mang oho* and their dead are obligatory
counsellors, esteemed above all others. The *yan ur* respect and fear
the *duad-nit* much more than their own house's dead, for the former
protect, punish and kill. A house's well-being is thus assured not
by its own dead but rather by the dead of all its *mang oho*. The latter's is the most highly venerated authority, since it is founded on
their relationship with the dead and the god. Moreover, while the
mang oho play the role of intermediaries between the *yan ur* and
the god, their own (that is, their house's) dead are usually honoured
not by them but rather by their exchange partners *yan ur*. It is as if
they were not in a position to venerate their dead alone, and could
do so through those toward whom their life, that is, their blood
has flowed, those who have received their daughters. Patrilineal
descent within a house appears to be less important than the de-
scending lines traversing houses, including all the descendants of
all the sisters who have gone forth from the house, and over whom
their *mang oho* conserve authority. While the offering to the spirits
mitu is meant to notify them of the bride's departure from her
house, a permanent institution which they protect, for the *duad-*

30. When a man marries his matrilateral cross-cousin, his *duad-nit* include the bride's father
himself.
31. A similar role as intermediary is also played by the spirits *mitu*, who, at the level of the
society *lór*, are considered 'the weapons of the god' who punish and kill.

nit the movement of their uterine descendants outside the house of origin assures their authority a certain permanence. Thus, although houses are permanent structures, exchanges impart movement to their content and, as we shall see, do much else besides.

The prestation of pigs to the spirits *mitu* bears the same name as the ritual offering of a rice cake and of bananas and chicken made to the ancestors and the god at various stages in the construction of a sailing-boat. An offering of pigs is also made, and given the same name, when an adopted child leaves his house of birth for his house of adoption. In our conclusion, we will have occasion to mention briefly the comparison frequently made by the villagers between Tanebar-Evav society and a sailing-boat. For the moment, it suffices to stress that prestations bearing the same name, although composed of completely different objects and addressed to different supernatural beings, are offered both in a relationship between two houses when a bride is given away, and in a relationship between two societies when a sailing-boat is sold. The internal relations of the society thus seem to be a subsystem of its relations with the outside world. Two levels of value should be distinguished here:

• Exchanges in which the parties are houses, individual units protected by the spirits *mitu*, who are the guardians of the society in its specificity. At this level, the whole composed by the houses and their ritual functions constitute *haratut*;
• Exchanges with the ancestors in general and with the god. These exchanges are associated with the completeness of the society *lór-haratut* symbolised by a sailing-boat. Nonetheless, the prestation of pigs called 'bananas–chicken', offered to the *mitu* at the marriage ceremony, bears the name of, and thus clearly makes reference to, the prestations offered during the construction of a sailing-boat.

The offering of the basket hung around the bridegroom's neck should be understood in reference to the two levels of value *haratut* and *lór-haratut*. Indeed, the insistent presence of half a whole (half of a leaf, one stone of a pair) marks an inversion of the opposition exterior–interior. We have already remarked that, in relation to the *mang oho* 'people of the village', the *yan ur* and thus the husband are seen as coming from outside. A proverb even compares a bridegroom to flotsam seeking an island (a wife) on which to wash ashore. But here the two fruits, which really do come from off the island and really were washed ashore, represent the female element. This inversion, as well as the incompleteness already noted, would seem to indicate that we are no longer at the same level of value as in the preceding ritual. The unity of the *yan ur – mang oho* relationship, connected with the values of *haratut*, is sealed by the betrotheds' eating the hard-boiled egg. It gives way here to a half-totality, represented by the husband alone, and an inversion of the relation exterior–interior. What is at stake is no longer the existence of houses as such, dependent upon exchanges between two marriage groups, but rather the relation between the values of *lór* and *haratut*. The connection of island society with the outside world is one aspect of this relation. The allusion to the myth and ritual of the launching of a sailing-boat (through the presence of one of the two small meteorites) suggests the idea of the society conceived of as a whole. We are still in the sphere of exchanges here, but at a completely different level, that of the relationship between *lór* and *haratut*.

The various prestations exchanged or offered at the marriage ceremony thus make reference to an order of values which transcends the simple organisation of marriages.

The prestation of a cannon and gongs which 'replace' the bride's body must be interpreted in conjunction with those which are offered in cases of murder, incest or adoption. In these latter situations, the social order has already been shattered or is at least imminently threatened. Money – conceived of in a local myth as related to the interior and origins, but in fact introduced from the outside world in exchange for sailing-boats or as the result of wars – functions as the operative element in a 'replacement' when either of the society's two values is concerned, *lór* in instances of murder and incest, and *haratut* in cases of adoption. It partakes of both values and bears in itself something of the whole. The *mang oho*, 'people of the village', confirm the importance of receiving from outside the money indispensable for the continued existence of the village, which the *yan ur*, conceived of as people from off the island, contribute. The *mang oho* seem able to acquire money only through the gift of their women, just as in the past money entered the society only as a result of the departure of sailing-boats.

The orientation of the exchanges in a marriage relationship, revealed in their movements, and the nature of these exchanges, should now be clearer. Along one vector, the god creates life and inflicts death through the intermediary of the *mang oho*. At this

level, the values of *haratut* are dominant. Along the opposite vector, the *yan ur* protect life by giving a key element of the container
necessary for its survival. In their very subordination to the values of *haratut*, however, it is they who recall the contrary values of
lór, the society turned toward the outside and protected by the law
of *lór*. Although the *yan ur* do not protect the container, they furnish its key element, thus marking their fundamental relationship
with the outside. In the exchange of prestations, the relationship
between *mang oho* and *yan ur* is organised as a hierarchical opposition in which the values of *haratut*, represented by the *mang oho*,
encompass the values of *lór*, associated with the *yan ur*.

At another level, the values are inverted, and direct us to the
society conceived of as a whole. Here, the prestations between
houses make reference to this whole, formed by the relation between *lór* and *haratut*, to the totality represented as a sailing-boat.

Exchanges for the rebirth of society

At Tanebar-Evav, exchanges of women cannot be isolated from the
numerous other sorts of exchanges which occur, and do not alone
provide an adequate basis for an interpretation of the social system. On the one hand, the rituals associated with marriage exchanges and the expressions employed there constantly allude both
to other types of exchanges and to the value system, that is, to the
society conceived of as a whole. On the other, inter-marriage itself
involves relationships and exchanges which extend beyond marriage and the life cycle of individuals.

While their continued existence is dependent on marriage and
adoption (which involve replacement), houses are at the same time
encompassed in the vaster movement of the entire society, understood as *haratut* or *lór*, in which they participate not in their own
names but as representatives of the whole. They no longer face each
other two by two in exchanges which, taken together, give a certain idea of the society. Grouped in entities which make reference
to the society as a totality, they enter into exchange relationships
with the god, the ancestors, the dead and other categories of supernatural beings, as well as with other societies of the same type.

If, for example, too much flotsam drifts ashore, or incest or some
other grave misdeed sullies a house, all the houses without excep-
tion must take part in purification ceremonies conducted in the

name of *lór*. Offerings to cleanse the village are made by the whole community to the spirit Hukum.

In olden times, when a case of incest between brother and sister was discovered, the guilty couple used to be thrown into the sea with stones tied about their necks. They received no funeral, and their wandering souls were believed to join those of beings who had disappeared at sea or in the forest. When such a case arises now, two sailing-boats stand out to sea, one bearing the guilty brother and sister, the other loaded with money of various sorts (a cannon, a gong, jewellery) which is to replace their bodies. When deep water is reached, the money on the second sailing-boat is thrown overboard, and the brother and sister are transferred to it from the first. The latter boat returns to port empty, to convince the spirits that the death sentence has been executed. The village must then be purified through a ceremony in which the men run about in a frenzy, killing any humans who have not taken refuge, slaughtering the animals they come across and destroying plants and trees. This ritual cleansing is called *sob lór*, 'to honour *lór*'. Not just the guilty house is concerned here, since the replacement is offered in the name of the entire society *lór* to the spirit Hukum, guardian of the law. This exchange not only saves the lives of the guilty couple, who may now participate in the usual interplay of exchanges, marry and have children, but also re-establishes the integrity of the society which the incestuous relationship had shattered.

A local proverb describes the result of incest: 'Water leaks into the hold of the sailing-boat, it drips from the ridge-pole of the house.' The reference to the names given the cannon offered as part of the marriage compensation, 'keel of the sailing-boat' or 'ridge-pole of the house', is clear. While marriage exchanges assure the completeness of a house, incest, which is the absence of exchange, signifies the deterioration of its key element. Houses and marriage are on the level of *haratut* and its values – relations with the god, origins, the society considered from the standpoint of its internal structure and identified with the *mang oho*. The society *lór* and its values are, in a sense, introduced negatively to guarantee the order of *haratut*, to protect it and to repair the damage caused by incest or other misdeeds. *Lór* does not act only as a guarantor, however. It also contributes positively to the maintenance of the social order. This is clear in another context, the ritual millet cultivation cycle, where the society *haratut* is seen to be indebted to *lór* for its continued existence and for the origin of life.

The annual millet cultivation cycle brings together the entire community around its initiated elders in a ritualised collective task punctuated by numerous ceremonies. It concludes with a gift by each individual of a part of his harvest to the common granary of *haratut*.

The Lord of the Land and the other initiated elders direct the millet rituals at every stage, from the clearing of the land to the harvest. Only after they have made the necessary offerings and begun their own gardens do the rest of the villagers set to work. A single tract of forest land is divided into individual plots and cultivated. The annual cycle is meant to bring about the village's rebirth, and requires a collective effort, *ót maren*,[32] to help the 'King of the Golden Mountain', who takes his name from the sacred place at the centre of the village, to be born again each year. A successful harvest brings renown everywhere to the King's (that is, to the village's) name. The objective of the agricultural and ritual work performed is described metaphorically as 'the progress of the sailing-boat with a good wind and calm seas'. Offerings are made to the god Sun–Moon, to the Earth-Mother, to the spirits *mitu* who protect the village, and to a particular category of supernatural beings called 'the disappeared'. All of them are asked to protect the work undertaken and to bring from outside good luck, millet, and pigs to be hunted down and offered before the harvest. The society *haratut* thus requests from outside the essential elements it needs to fill its granary and be reborn.

The 'disappeared' are the spirits of persons who, after a quarrel or misdeed offensive to Hukum, went off into the forest and never returned, or who drowned at sea and whose bodies were never recovered. In either case, they have never received a proper funeral, and are said to inhabit certain specific places in the forest, as well as on a small neighbouring desert island called Nuhuta. At different stages of the millet cultivation cycle, each officiant makes offerings in the forest to certain of the 'disappeared' with whom his house is connected. While the dead in general are offered rice in small plaited bags made from coconut palm leaves, the 'disappeared' are given bags of the same sort, but empty,

---

32. *Ot maren* is collective work organised by an individual to help him, for example, to construct his house or his sailing-boat. It may involve his immediate family alone, or various related houses, or even the entire village. He offers a meal to his helpers, and they in turn generally contribute a 'present of food', *yelim* (*hadya* in Indonesian), in addition to their labour. Both men and women participate.

together with empty bean pods and tuber peelings. This offering is called *ót lenar*. The king of the 'disappeared' is asked to distribute this semblance of food among them and to see to it that they do not quarrel over it. During the same period, the god, the spirits Adat and Hukum, and sometimes even 'foreign' spirits are also invoked and are offered a sort of sham money, tin scrapings called 'gold'. If the 'disappeared' were not fed, small parasites and other insects would destroy the harvest. It would then be said that *lór* had taken its part, leaving nothing for the villagers.

Before the millet is sown, the Lord of the Land makes an offering in the name of the entire village to 'replace' the plants and animals (snakes, mice, insects and so forth) 'killed' during the clearing of the forest, which are said to 'belong to *lór*'. This prestation is a payment to the spirit Hukum, and is analogous to that made in the case of murder, where the victim is replaced by money. If a sailing-boat returns from Nuhuta during the period when gardens are being prepared, the following day it is forbidden to set foot in the gardens. This obligatory day of rest is meant to honour the souls of the 'disappeared', which are believed to have followed the sailing-boat, and which otherwise would take their revenge by sending snakes, mice and lizards to eat the new millet shoots. The offerings to the 'disappeared' are thus in part preventive, since the villagers must feed them to avoid their serving themselves.

Another ritual sequence illustrates a more positive aspect of the 'disappeared'. Offerings are made and a ceremony with songs and dances is performed in their honour and, in particular, in honour of their king, whom the villagers entreat to send rain before the sowing begins. It is he who asks the wind to blow, bringing rain to prepare the soil. We should recall, in this connection, the two black oblong stones, the testicles of the rain or the tornado, which fell to earth after an overly violent copulation with the clouds. The rain is thus clearly a masculine element which fecundates the earth. These stones appear in two rituals, at marriages and in the ceremonies for the maiden voyage of a sailing-boat (see below). Together, they are a symbol of completeness.

The rain, requested from the king of the 'disappeared' who is associated with *lór*, must fecundate the Earth-Mother so that she can give birth to the King of the Golden Mountain. The specific task of *haratut*, the village society, is to aid the King of the Golden Mountain, who is one with the village and the society, to be reborn, that is, to help the millet grow by means of the ritual work performed, including the ritual hunt for wild pigs just before the harvest. When the grain is ready to be reaped, the men go into the forest to kill seven wild pigs, which are offered to the five principal guardian spirits (*mitu*) of the village, to the god and to the dead. All this ritual work taken together, the millet cultivation ceremonies and the hunt, is the *maren* for the King of the Golden Mountain. The King's rebirth each year (a successful harvest) glorifies his name and the society's. The pigs are offered both to give thanks for the harvest and to magnify the King's name. It is said simply that the society now has a 'name'.

These tasks, associated with the society *haratut* (since it is *haratut*'s common granary that must be filled), thus depend for their success on the society *lór*, which, however, also represents a constant threat to the whole enterprise. From *lór* come the 'disappeared', who, unlike the other dead, have not received the funeral which would permit their bodies to rejoin the earth and their souls to disperse. The *yan ur* and the *mang oho* of their houses did not complete the cycle of exchanges begun with them since, for lack of a proper funeral, those generally effectuated at death could not be carried out. We pass here from the level of inter-house exchanges, which the 'disappeared' have quit, to the highest level of the exchange cycle, which links the society *lór* to the society *haratut*. In this cycle *haratut* profits from the renown of *lór*, while remaining completely dependent on *lór* for its own survival and renown. In the passage from one level to another, the souls of the 'disappeared' may be envisioned schematically as leaving the inter-house exchange cycle, level *haratut*, and entering, not as individuals but as elements belonging to the society *lór*, the higher cycle of exchanges which consists of a circulation between *lór* and *haratut*.

A parallel may be drawn between the millet cultivation ceremonies and those performed when a child is born. In the latter case, the *yan ur*, 'children-sister', considered as masculine and as coming from outside, are the fecundating principle assuring, through their descendants, the perpetuation of the *duad-nit* who terrorise them and whom they venerate. Soon after birth, a child must be given a name. The men of the house, including the father, go to sea to catch fish and hunt tortoises, and their take is then consumed by the infant's *duad-nit* and the village elders at a ceremonial meal. The villagers say that the men have 'gone to seek a name [for the child] in the sea'. The masculine principle, which comes from outside, fecundates the woman, who is from inside, and, after a sea hunt, a name is given to the product of the seed which has been sown, the child who will permit the house to perpetuate itself and to maintain its place in the society's exchanges. In the case of millet, a masculine principle which comes from outside, the rain, associated with the society *lór*, fecundates the inside, the soil of the island, *haratut*, and thus permits the annual rebirth of the King of the Mountain, that is, of the millet. The King's (the village's) name is proclaimed after a ritual hunt, not at sea for tortoises and fish to be offered to the *duad-nit*, but in the forest (outside the village) for wild pigs to be offered to the *mitu*, the village's guardian spirits, who are for the most part said to have come from outside, as well as to the god and to all the village's dead.

The close association between the yearly rebirth of the village and of millet is clearly reflected in certain prohibitions imposed at Tanebar-Evav while millet is being cultivated. Noisemaking is forbidden so as not to awaken the millet, which is still young. The village may not be defiled by blood; if a pig is to be killed for a feast, it must be slaughtered outside the village walls. Just before the harvest, the surrounding island societies are advised when the ritual hunt will take place, so that while it is under way no boat will arrive and jeopardise its success. The island effectively closes up upon itself as if to protect what it is conceiving and, once the hunt is over, opens up again to proclaim its name.

After the birth of a child, the mother remains confined in her house until the day she goes to purify herself in the sea, at a point just outside the wall marking the entrance to the village harbour. It is as if she were herself leaving the womb formed by the village enclosure. Later on the same day, the newborn child is carried to the threshold of its house and presented to the village by a woman who, rocking it in her arms, cries: 'It's a boy!' or 'It's a girl!'.

The millet cultivation ritual thus consists of a cycle of exchanges not between units like houses, but rather between the living and certain supernatural beings, some of the latter associated with the values of *haratut*, and others with those of *lór*. In these exchanges, certain important elements come from outside to nourish and bring about the rebirth of the King of the Golden Mountain, who is the spirit of both millet and village society: pigs, millet, souls, and the aid of the 'disappeared' who are associated with *lór* (the fecundating rain requested from their king). With the annual rebirth represented by the millet harvest, the ultimate goal of the cycle is

attained – to be able to proclaim the name of the King of the Golden
Mountain outside the village, that is, before *lór*, the society in relation to the outside, including the various other villages of the Kei
archipelago. The society *lór* is thus implicated in two sorts of actions. The first have as their starting-point the acts of individuals
(murder, incest and adultery) which nonetheless always have collective consequences. The second affect the entire village from the
start, for example the most important rituals and the neutralisa-
tion of the danger represented by flotsam which washes ashore,
and also have collective consequences.

Individuals as such thus never take part in exchanges at Tanebar-
Evav. They only participate in them as members of some larger
unit, of a house or a group of houses when *haratut* is concerned,
or as members of the society as a whole when it is a question of
lór-haratut. This appears clearly in the millet cultivation ritual,
where both values are at work in the reconstruction of the cosmic
order, the all-embracing society of the living and the dead. The
dead and supernatural beings watch over the living, who in return
continue to honour them with offerings in a ceaselessly repeated
cycle. The ritual work performed at Tanebar-Evav, always explicitly conceived of as a return, constitutes the society's essential concern, since it ensures this continual circulation from life to death,
and from death to life.

*

The contrast between marriage exchanges and rituals, on the one
hand, and the circulation between *lór* and *haratut*, briefly studied
in the case of millet cultivation, on the other, calls for several observations.

Exchanges of women seem indeed to unfold at a level of value
where the society *haratut* is dominant. Each house is exclusively
either *yan ur* or *mang oho* with regard to the other houses with
which it has a marriage relationship. In each such relationship, the
mang oho are superior, associated with the origins of society and
the initial foundation of houses, and conceived of as intermediaries
between the *yan ur* and 'the god–the dead', the *duad-nit*. The units
created by exchange, the houses, are to be understood at this level.
They ensure the circulation of both life and death toward the *yan
ur*. *Mang oho* give life, in the form of children and sisters, who assure the perpetuation of the *yan ur*'s line, but can also inflict death,

like the god and the spirits Adat and Hukum.[33] *Yan ur*, on the other hand, through their offerings of money, which comes from the outside world, assure the completeness of their *mang oho*'s social unit, and honour them by their constant invocation of the *duad-nit* in all matters affecting their own house.[34]

When *yan ur* 'let the *duad-nit* gorge themselves' *(flurut duad-nit)*, they 'replace' a body lost to the *mang oho* by marriage or death. In the same way, in cases of war, incest or murder, bodies are 're-placed' by money. *Yan ur*, conceived of as coming from outside – in contrast with *mang oho* 'people of the village', but in the same way as flotsam ('flotsam seeks an island', as a husband seeks a wife) – are thus associated with the values of the society *lór*. At the level of exchanges of women and marriage exchanges, the values of *haratut* and *lór* are therefore both involved, but the former are domi-nant, as the *mang oho*'s position and their association with the *duad-nit* reveal.

This proposition establishes the exact place in the society's ide-ology of marriage exchanges, of the parties thereto, *yan ur* and *mang oho*, and of the houses founded in large part on exchange. On this ideological level, the society's values assume a particular configu-ration which does not, however, account for the society as a total-ity. The word 'level' is used here to designate such a specific ordering of values. The existence of different levels of value and the shifts from one level to another do not imply that the values in question vary, but rather that at a given level they are related to one another differently, each in turn assuming a dominant or sub-ordinated position in accordance with the level considered. The millet cultivation ritual, where the ordering of values observed at marriages is inverted, unfolds at a higher level of value.

We have seen that there is more to marriage at Tanebar-Evav than a simple exchange of women. This aspect is in a sense sec-ondary to another, which was brought to light by our discussion of marriage rituals and of the relationship with the dead, the *duad-nit*, and which implicitly incorporates a reference to the society as a totality, *lór-haratut*, likened to a sailing-boat.

Our description of the central ritual of the marriage ceremony

---

33. This is particularly true of the first *mang oho*. The house which, in the beginning, gave the first woman in marriage is called *mang oho itin kan*, which means literally: 'the foot of the millet stalk stripped of its grain'.

34. The ancestors of a hypothetical *mang oho* without *yan ur* would receive no offerings spe-cifically in their honour, but would only share in those presented by the entire society to the *nit* in general.

(the hanging of the small basket around the bridegroom's neck) revealed a certain number of inversions with regard to the configuration of values which is generally dominant in the exchanges between *mang oho* and *yan ur*. The basket, we recall, contains among other things, two fruits washed ashore, one of which is vulviform, and a stone which fell from the sky, said to be one of the testicles of the rain. From a ritual standpoint, it would seem that the union of male and female requires the presence of something from outside. The woman, not the *yan ur*, is here associated with the values of *lór*, while the man is linked to the sky and the god, which is normally the *mang oho*'s position.[35]

This passage through the outside implicitly makes reference to the society's superior values, to the encompassing of the values of *haratut* by those of *lór*, as we have shown in a prior article devoted to the sailing-boat and its occupants, image of the society in its totality and completeness (Barraud 1985). The two principal marriage rituals, the hanging of the basket around the bridegroom's neck and the offering of pigs to the houses' guardian spirits *mitu*, allude, each in its own way, to the sailing-boat ritual.

While at the marriage ceremony only one of the two stones which fell from the sky is present, both are necessary when a sailing-boat makes its maiden voyage. One is left on shore, watched over ceremonially by a young girl, while the other goes to sea with the boat, where it is cared for on board by a young boy. These stones, the testicles of the rain, are masculine symbols *par excellence*. The union of the masculine and feminine principles in a single whole is thus achieved the first time a sailing-boat puts out to sea, but the masculine value – dominant outside, and associated with *lór*, fecundation, rain and the *yan ur* – is clearly encompassing.

The other principal ritual of the marriage ceremony is the offering of pigs to the houses' guardian spirits *mitu*, to advise them that the bride has left her house of birth and now belongs to her husband's house. The name of this prestation, as we have already noted, recalls that of the one offered to the god and the ancestors when a sailing-boat is being built, which consists of a rice cake and 'chicken gruel' made from chicken, bananas (the latter cooked in the same way as a pig), and coconuts. At Tanebar-Evav, the construction of a sailing-boat is an element of one of the society's

35. Tornadoes, the 'penis of the rain' whose testicles fell to earth, are considered calamities, like epidemic diseases, which the god sends to punish men's misdeeds. They are often said to be the god's 'weapon'.

myths.[36] In the sailing-boat ritual, two carved sago palm figurines, representing the boy and the girl of the myth, are placed inside the boat during a divination ceremony and the meal which follows. At this meal, the men, seated in the unfinished hull, consume the offering. The women who prepared the rice cake must on the contrary remain outside the hull, so as not to jeopardise the boat's future safety. Men thus preside at the 'birth' of a sailing-boat, and women participate only secondarily. Small rice balls, 'the children of the rice cake', are placed on the three timbers supporting the hull, said to be its mother. Both the masculine and feminine principles are again at work, the former here in a dominant position. The myth itself tells the story of a sort of inverted conception and birth, compared to that of a child or of millet, since in it the masculine principle, associated with the land, is fecundated by the feminine principle, which comes from the sky. This inversion of the values of *haratut* implies that here the ordering of the society's values is different, and that those of *lór* are dominant. At Tanebar-Evav, furthermore, the society as a whole, *lór-haratut*, is constantly compared to a sailing-boat navigating at sea with its occupants. The titles of the elders who exercise the principal ritual and political functions in the society are derived from those used to designate a boat's principal officers. The chief elder, head of the entire society, is 'Sea Captain', and two 'Land Captains' follow him in order of precedence.

This comparison is confirmed, on another plane of analysis, by the names given to the different parts of a sailing-boat and the terms used to describe its structure. A boat is likened to a human body. Its backbone is said to be its keel, whose middle section is masculine, while its two extremities, forming the bow and the stern, are feminine. The two meeting-points of these three pieces are called 'the interstices between the penis and the vagina'. The hull's principal planks bear the names of different parts of the human body, including even the arteries. Finally, the optimal waterline is called 'the juncture of the living and the dead'.

36. The myth may be summarised briefly as follows. A man was building his sailing-boat on the beach when some blood fell from the sky into an earthenware pot near him. The next day he heard crying and, on looking into the pot, saw a child who was crying for his mother. They both decided to go look for her in the sky. When they got there, they found a woman who had had a miscarriage. She recognised her child and decided to marry the 'father', who then remained in the sky. Two children, a boy and a girl (the myth does not tell whether they are the couple's children or whether they are brother and sister), descended to the earth to watch over the sailing-boat.

Numerous other examples could be cited to show that the sailing-boat is an image of completeness and of the whole. It is the society, composed of the living and the dead, protected by the sea and at its mercy, just as the society *haratut* is protected by *lór* and at its mercy. At Tanebar-Evav, the delivery of a child is compared to a sailing-boat's progress through the harbour channel which leads it to deep water. The dead are buried with their feet toward the sea, to enable them to leave for the island of the dead.

These brief observations concerning the sailing-boat permit us to perceive more clearly why an understanding of marriage exchanges and rituals requires reference to the society as a whole, and to the encompassment of the values of *haratut* by those of *lór*. This encompassment is at work in the millet cultivation rituals, through which the entire society brings about its annual rebirth through the circulation of beings and 'things' from *lór* to *haratut* and from *haratut* to *lór*. Marriage exchanges only assume their full meaning as part of the general circulation between these two sets of fundamental values which define the society. It could be said that the exchanges of women and prestations are caught up in a vaster circulation which sustains and perpetuates them. *Lór* protects against internal misdeeds (incest, murder and adultery) by meting out punishment for them, just as it protects against flotsam, whose arrival destroys Tanebar-Evav's inner harmony, by publicly ratifying its entry into island society. It is the community's response to individual events which interfere with the relations between the social units of *haratut*.

A few words are in order, in conclusion, concerning the *duad-nit*. By their ties to the god and to origins (in particular to the origin of houses), they are associated with the values of *haratut*. From another viewpoint, however, as maternal uncles and holders of authority, as those who give life and inflict death, they are also connected with the values of *lór*. It is said that the spirit Hukum, the law, to whom offerings are made when the society *lór* acts, considers the society as his 'nephews'. *Lór* inflicts punishment but also contributes fecundating elements from the outside world. The *duad-nit* thus appear to be at the juncture of the values of *haratut* and *lór*. They permit the transition from a general structure of male–female complementarity in which the masculine principle is dominant, to an affinity structure where the feminine principle prevails. They are, like the brother–sister relationship, a point of passage from a universal (male–female completeness represented by the sailing-boat) to particularity (the affinity structure). The referent for the sailing-boat is not the husband–wife couple but rather a boy and a girl. The *duad-nit*, associated with both the living and the dead, with the god and with punishment, give meaning to a specific marriage system in the framework of a particular society's hierarchy of values. The explanatory force of asymmetric marriage at Tanebar-Evav resides in the additional confirmation it provides of this hierarchy, since it appears the most adequate means of bringing into play the society's fundamental values. It should be seen as deriving from the value system, not as its source.

IV. Iqar'iyen

We begin here by analysing the exchanges characterising the system of honour, then discuss those in which both honour and *baraka* are involved. In conclusion, we touch briefly on the aspects of *baraka* which transcend exchange and relate directly to the universal nature of Islam.

Exchanges in the system of honour

Honour, for individuals and groups, consists in exercising authority over certain 'forbidden domains' and, where exchanges of violence are concerned, in transgressing the taboo attached to others' forbidden domains.

Understood as the exercise of authority over forbidden domains, honour has both a collective and an individual dimension. On the one hand, every segmentary group – the confederation of Iqar'iyen tribes, as well as each tribe, fraction of a tribe, territorial community, quarter associated with a particular patrilineal group and, finally, each household – has a territory to defend. On the other, each householder can claim the status of a man of honour (*ariaz*) if he has a wife and, even more important, owns land. These two dimensions, collective and individual, are related, but not reciprocally, since anything which affects the honour of an individual reflects on that of his group but the opposite is not necessarily true. Thus, for example, a threat to a householder's land is also directed against his group's territory. On the contrary, an attack on a group's common well by another group may only lead to a struggle between the two groups as such, without also involving inter-individual conflicts. This imbalance results from the fact that a householder's land is included within his group's territory, not the reverse.

Claude Lefort, in another context, has coined a phrase which nicely sums up honour understood as the exchange of violence: 'One does not give in order to receive, one gives so that the other will give' (1978: 27). In Iqar'iyen society, exchanges of violence assume three forms: oratorical bouts, lavish conspicuous spending, and physical violence. All three may be said to be violent, however, since each can lead to the death, real or symbolic, of men of honour. These exchanges, which always involve challenge and counter-challenge, are transgressive forms of behaviour that confirm the existence of a forbidden domain by violating it and casting doubt on a householder's or a group's authority. Transgressions of this sort do not, however, fundamentally challenge the value system, since a man of honour only attacks something worthy of him. A challenger oversteps the limits but, by his very act, recognises the value of what he transgresses.

Of these three forms of exchange, murder is the most important and lends a violent overtone to the other two as well. Oratorical bouts are provocations which can result in dishonour, in symbolic death. Lavish conspicuous spending supposes a host's giving his numerous guests great quantities of things to 'eat' at ceremonies and feasts, and a generous man always runs the risk of ruining himself, of being forced to sell his land and go into exile or of becoming someone else's dependant. Words and goods are here substitutes for men, and the real stake is the existence of the men themselves as men of honour.

Murder, and exchanges of physical violence in general, are the most dangerous but also the most elaborately organised form of exchange. Every man of honour knows that he tempts death when he decides to enter the realm of violence, but he knows also that such perils are unavoidable if he wishes others to recognise his worth. As one informant put it: 'Here, a man of honour, an *ariaz*, has his courage, his daring and his rifle or he really isn't a man.' Violence is exercised in adherence to strict rules which vary with the types of groups confronting each other. Exchanges of violence between high-level segmentary groups should be distinguished from those between patrilineal groups, whatever their segmentary distance.

(a) Exchanges of violence between segmentary groups
When such a group organises a raid, it steals its adversary's live-
stock and grain, but tries to avoid taking human life. The group
that has been attacked then responds with a similar raid. After this
exchange, the groups may decide to return the stolen goods to each
other. If tempers are up, however, which is frequently the case, they
may have a battle, which is fought in an open place, in stages determined by well-established rules. First, the young men of each
group swagger forward, vaunting their group's honour and dis-
paraging that of their adversaries. Then, after everyone has care-
fully taken cover, all the men begin to hurl stones and shoot rifles
at one another. After a time, *shorfa* mediators intervene suddenly,
come between the two parties, calm tempers and persuade them
to settle their conflict peacefully. The stolen goods are returned, and
violence is suspended until the next incident. A battle is thus a sort
of mock combat in which the groups involved foster their reciprocal animosity by very ritualised, and only very rarely deadly,
violence. If a man does happen to be killed, the patrilineal groups
on each side intervene and settle the matter in the manner described below. By means of these raids and battles, the segmentary groups periodically stir up their chronic hostility, whose
origins are lost in the mists of time, and reanimate the entire segmentary structure through an endless chain of acts of ritualised violence.

(b) Exchanges of violence between patrilineal groups
Exchanges of violence between hostile patrilineal groups do not
take into account their segmentary distance, and unfold quite differently from those just considered. They involve honour on two
planes, that of the groups and that of individual householders.
Murders or attempted murders arise from conflicts concerning
land or women. While in a battle between segmentary groups 'irresponsible' young men play the most visible role, exposing themselves unprotected to their adversaries, here the initiative is taken
by an *ariaz*, a man of honour, who lies in wait for his adversary in
the mountains and uses all his cunning to kill him. After committing his murder, he must spring up and throw his rifle into the air.
With this essential gesture, he signs his and, consequently, his
group's challenge. The victim's closest agnate must then respond
by a counter-challenge, that is, by another murder, to avenge his
family's and his patrilineal group's honour. If he wavers in his re-

solve, a more distant agnate may supplant him, depriving him of his vengeance. In this case, the more distant relative increases his prestige, while the honour of the close relative who failed to act is seriously impaired. In either event, the counter-challenge must strike down either the initial murderer or one of his agnates. The exchanges of murder should come to an halt when each death or injury on one side is matched by a death or injury on the other. Both groups' honour having been restored, public opinion glorifies the men of honour who distinguished themselves, and ridicules those who shrank from danger. Other similar exchanges inevitably follow, however, since, in this society, it is intolerable that some men's honour remain greater than others'. Those who have proven their daring will sooner or later be challenged anew by men from their own group or from other patrilineal groups who wish in turn to assert their honour. Violence thus follows upon violence in an endless sequence, and a man's prestige is always precarious.

An ambitious man may succeed in imposing his pre-eminence within his patrilineal group and become a 'great man' (*amghar*, plural *imgharen*), a man of honour *par excellence*, who takes on the responsibility for defending his entire group's honour. He is incessantly obliged to reaffirm his authority over his lineage, to spend lavishly and to respond to challenges. Such a man's position is always highly unstable, and his struggle to maintain it may well cost him his life. When he dies, his authority is not inherited by his son, and every man in his patrilineal group then recovers the right to resolve his own and his group's problems of honour for himself.

Chart 4 synthesises and contrasts the different forms assumed by the exchanges of violence characterising the system of honour. These exchanges may be analysed from two different perspectives. From one, they all manifest a certain sort of reciprocity. From another, however, they may be seen as unfolding on two different, hierarchically ordered levels.

For the partners to an exchange, equivalence or even exact equality between what is given and what is returned is the rule. If one receives a meal or a gift, one must offer the giver a similar meal or gift. In the same way, a violent act calls for an equivalent violent act – a raid provokes a raid, a murder a murder. Contrary to what might be expected, however, this principle of reciprocity does not imply that the series of exchanges will, in the long run, come to a halt. It has, rather, the contrary effect. Raids in series thus never

CHART 4

EXCHANGES	between segmentary groups	between patrilineal groups without regard to their segmentary distance
The partners	Segmentary groups without regard to their internal differentiation	Lineages and householders
Types of confrontation	Feuding and periodic raids	Murders in endless series
Formalized temporary settlement	Ritualized battles	A violent act responds to and settles a prior violent act
Result	No differentiation of groups in terms of honour	Differentiation, especially among householders

succeed in settling definitively the dispute which has opposed two segmentary groups from time immemorial and which, despite periods of peace, will sooner or later be invoked to justify the resumption of the exchanges of violence. In the same way, murder follows murder in an infinite series, although the partners to the exchanges change. Indeed, it seems that the specific partners are less important than an overriding obligation to go on exchanging endlessly.

Our analysis leads us to take a resolutely hierarchical view of the exchanges characterising the system of honour. On a lower level, a competition for prestige underlies the exchanges between patrilineal groups. Cunning and strategy are important for the ambitious men who seek to establish their pre-eminence within their own group and their renown throughout the society. An obligation to respond is the rule, although the form it takes varies with the social position of the partners. If an inferior challenges a 'great man', the latter may only respond through the intermediary of one of his own clients. At the end of each exchange, the result is a gain or loss in prestige for each of the partners.

This level of competition is, however, subordinated to another where the exchanges, unfolding in an endless series, weave the very fabric of tribal society. No durable 'accumulation of symbolic capital', to use P. Bourdieu's concept, is possible among the Iqar'iyen. Prestige and authority are always finally brought low, and each single, reciprocal exchange is subsumed in a sort of piling up of rash but necessary acts, be they gifts or murders. For, in this society's values, gifts and murders alike are metaphorical forms of ingestion which open the way to transformations of a higher order, where *baraka* plays a decisive role (see Section 2 below). On this higher level of honour, the partners themselves cease to be the points of reference, and honour is only secondarily a value incarnated in individuals or groups. It is, more fundamentally, the value characterising the general system of exchanges of violence. One is, here, beyond individual honour, beyond prestige or authority and, finally, beyond closed binary reciprocity.

Exchanges and the relation between honour and *baraka*

Our study of exchanges of violence has revealed a system of relations centred on the giving of death. Other exchanges exist, how-

ever, which transform a gift of death into a gift of life. Beginning
with a murder, they are settled through a compensatory payment
to the victim's agnates. It is no longer a question here of honour
alone, but also and above all of the relation between honour and
baraka, which as a manifestation of divine power is a source of life.
In these cases, *shorfa*, men recognised as descendants of the
prophet, certain of whom are said to have received *baraka* or the
'divine blessing', intervene as mediators. They form distinct lineages, each of which inhabits its own territory called a *horm*, a 'forbidden domain [under the authority of God]'. Essentially pacific,
the *shorfa* cannot themselves be challenged, and their *horm* are
sanctuaries from violence. They are venerated, on the contrary,
precisely for the divine virtue they possess. Their mediation is required in battles between segmentary groups, or when a man has
been killed.

In the latter case, various motives are adduced by informants
to explain why one or both of the patrilineal groups involved
wished to break off the exchanges of violence. All of them may,
however, be reduced to an individual fear of death or a group fear
of extermination. The parties first establish contact secretly with a
sherif of the *baraka*. The initial negotiations are delicate and must
remain strictly confidential, since doubt would be cast on the pe-
titioning groups' honour and on the *sherif*'s *baraka* if he were finally
to fail in his mission. A *sherif* is neither judge nor arbiter, and cannot impose his decisions, which must be freely accepted by the parties to the conflict. His intervention is only made public once he
has probed the real intentions of both camps, and the adversary
groups, which may not show their fear, have let him understand
by discreet allusions that they are prepared to accept a pacific settlement.

The *sherif* then determines, subject to both parties' consent, the
nature of the *diyith* ('blood money') to be offered by the murderer
to his victim's family. Generally he must pay a sum of money, but
may sometimes be obliged instead to give a woman to the offended
group in marriage or, very rarely, to work for them himself as a
servant. The latter two solutions are extremely humiliating for the
murderer's group, which will accept them only if it has few men
left and fears complete extermination. They imply a group's definitive, or at least prolonged, elimination from the competition for
honour. The first solution, a monetary payment, is, on the contrary,
seen as less one-sided, and gives rise to intense, exacting negotia-

tions. If the sum finally agreed upon is high, public opinion holds that the victim's group has demonstrated its sense of honour and has humbled the murderer by obliging him to pay for his act dearly. If it is small, the victim's agnates' prestige is tarnished, while the murderer's is enhanced. Even the payment of a murder compensation thus gives rise to competition among the Iqar'iyen. The amount of the *diyith* is not pre-established, and the sum of 'blood money' finally paid is the measure of each group's honour.

Once agreement on the *diyith* has been reached, a peace ritual seals the reconciliation. The murderer, his hands bound behind his back and a knife between his teeth, walks toward his victim's group's territory. The members of his patrilineal group, accompanied by the *sherif* of the *baraka*, follow behind him in a long procession, bringing with them the blood money as well as a sheep and various condiments. Soon after they enter their adversaries' territory, a close agnate of the victim comes forward to meet them, takes the knife from between the murderer's teeth, unties his hands, and proceeds to cut the sheep's throat (*dbiha*). This ritual act, by which the victim's agnates accept an animal as a substitute for the murderer, is called *'ar*. Once it has been performed, they may no longer take vengeance on him, for they would be smitten by a divine curse. The *sherif* then blesses those present, declaring that peace will bring them prosperity and wealth, and the sacrificed sheep is roasted and shared by both groups at a meal they take together. In gratitude for his services, the *sherif* is then given 'presents' (*hediya*), in kind or in money.

The mediation is thus the crucial moment when the transition is made from exchanges of violence to the peace of God, when honour gives way to *baraka*. Nonetheless, it carries within it the seeds of renewed violence. These two consequences are foreshadowed both in the payment of 'blood money' and in the ritual act *'ar*.

The decision to pay a *diyith*, while it temporarily puts a halt to exchanges of murder, displaces the competition to the negotiations over the blood money and, as we have seen, setting this sum is far from simple. But, what is more, for the Iqar'iyen only a new murder victim really has the same value as a previous one, and the recourse to blood money casts doubt on both lineages' honour. The murderer's group has recoiled after throwing down a challenge, while the victim's has accepted the replacement of their dead agnate by a poor substitute, a sheep. On the level of honour, the peace of God is only a truce and, after a pause, the exchanges of violence will resume in one form or another. Nonetheless, this irruption of peace, this truce however fleeting, bears witness to the divine power which induces men of honour to wish to submit to *baraka*. *Baraka* manifests itself here as the ultimate value, completely subordinating honour. The peace ritual reveals, in all its might, the fundamental reason for the success of the mediation.

In this ritual, the *'ar* is the essential moment. The Arabic word itself means both 'sacrifice' and 'shame'. The cutting of the sheep's throat in place of that of the murderer who has offered himself as victim is an explicit reference to the story of Abraham and Isaac. Symbolically, the murderer becomes a sort of son for his victim's agnates and succeeds in transforming their forbidden domain *haram* into a sanctuary *horm*, where he is safe from vengeance. Other circumstances exist in which an *'ar* intervenes, in different guises but always with similar consequences. By sacrificing a sheep before the door of an eminent man of honour's house, or by using cunning to slip into his house and seise hold of the millstone (a woman's implement), or take refuge in his wife's skirts, or suckle at her breast, a hunted man can transform the man of honour's *haram* into a *horm* where he is safe from vengeance. This behaviour, far from manifesting aggressiveness, denotes submission to a 'father' and consequently to the ultimate value, *baraka*.

The term *'ar* also means 'shame', and is interpreted in this sense on the level of honour. The murderer has abdicated as a man of honour, humbling himself before the very persons he had challenged and acquiescing on humiliating terms to becoming their 'son', an irresponsible young man. But the victim's agnates have also dishonoured themselves, by agreeing to accept the murderer symbolically as their son instead of taking his life for his crime. In order for both sides to cleanse themselves of their shame, the exchanges of violence, when they eventually revive, will assume even greater intensity.

In the peace ritual, however, the feeling of shame is temporarily subordinated to the sacrifice's acknowledged power to transform the gift of death into a gift of life. An animal victim, as in the story of Abraham and Isaac, is substituted for the murderer, who symbolically assumes the role of his victim's son. The Divinity, even in receiving this new victim, restores life, and the blessing of the *sherif* who presides over the entire ritual offers a further guarantee of this transformation. Does he not promise prosperity and progeny to both parties?

A few remarks may be useful to clarify the various dimensions of this return to life.

• The sacrifice *'ar* must be accomplished on the murder victim's territory, before his house, that is, in his *haram* or forbidden domain which, initially a place of honour, now becomes the domain of *baraka*, a sanctuary, *horm*, where violence is prohibited. The forbidden domain is rendered fertile by the divine force of *baraka*, which thus assures the perpetuation of Iqar'iyen society.

• This form of exchange does not suppose the equivalence of what is given and what is received, of the *sherif*'s services, in particular the ritual services he performs, and the presents he is offered. Similarly, the blood money does not replace the murder victim. Where honour is in question, 'return' has a single meaning: what is given back for a gift or a murder must be rigorously identical to what was received. The *diyith*, however, has two fundamental meanings, which, cannot be placed on the same level. It is the price of honour, but also the price of *baraka*. The agreement to pay a *diyith* opens the way to the sacrificial ritual which consecrates the hierarchical superiority of *baraka*, the ultimate value, over honour, which at other times governs relations among the tribesmen.

• The contrast between the endless exchanges of gifts and murders on the level of honour, and the hierarchically superior transformation, through *baraka*, of a gift of death into a gift of life, makes it clear that while honour shapes men's destinies, it only leads them on to destruction and can never in itself regenerate life. Only the divine force of *baraka*, by rendering fertile men's forbidden domains, can periodically, though only temporarily, put a halt to the implacable succession of murders and, by subordinating honour, reintroduce life. The supremacy of *baraka* nonetheless manifests itself only after a murder has already been committed. The killing of a victim would seem to be a necessary precondition to the transformation operated by *baraka*.

The close relationship which exists between destructive violence and the peace of God will be clearer after a brief analysis of the status of the Sultan of Morocco.

The coins struck by the Makhzen, the Moroccan authorities, bear the Sultan's seal and, for the Iqar'iyen, symbolise the ruler himself. In commercial transactions, debts may be settled in this or other sorts of money of French or Spanish origin. Only these Moroccan coins may be used, however, in the payment of blood money and, there, the fact that they symbolise the Moroccan sovereign is significant.

Since the seventeenth century, the Sultan has always issued from a particular lineage of *shorfa*, the Alawites, and he alone allies violence and *baraka* in his actions. The Iqar'iyen show themselves very conscious of this unique quality when they relate how a new Sultan comes to the throne. In Morocco, the order of royal succession is not fixed, and each new sovereign must defeat his rivals, suppress the anarchy which generally follows upon his predecessor's death, and re-establish the pre-existing order founded on the divine Law of Islam. The pretender must 'eat' the tribes which have entered into 'rebellion' (*siba*) by plundering them, devastating their land and beheading the principal rebel leaders. Only after emerging victorious from these tests does he accede to the throne. His violence is then perceived as a manifestation of *baraka* which will touch the entire Moroccan community, rendering fertile both women and land.

The Sultan's dual and apparently contradictory character casts light on the exclusive use of coins symbolically representing him in the payment of the blood money which permits a transition from exchanges of murder to the peace of God. In the local context of the Iqar'iyen tribes, and in that of Morocco as a whole, certain parallel sequences and transformations may be observed:

• *local context* : a murder ♦ *sherif*'s mediation ♦ payment of blood money to the victim's agnates + sacrifice *'ar* + presents offered to the *sherif* ♦ peace of God + fecundation of forbidden domains by *baraka* ♦ (after a time) resumption of exchanges of violence.
• *Morocco as a whole* : Sultan's death ♦ anarchy and rebellion ♦ pretender to the throne vanquishes his rivals and 'eats' the rebel tribes ♦ his victory is a victory of *baraka* ♦ the divine order is re-established and reigns once again in the Moroccan community ♦ the new sovereign's *baraka* fecundates women and land ♦ (after a time) death of the new Sultan and new violent interregnum.

In each case, the ultimate value *baraka* erupts into and transforms the system of relations through the intervention of a descendant of the Prophet, the *sherif* or the pretender. Their actions, in both cases, bear witness to the presence of a hierarchy of values. The price of honour is subordinated to the price of *baraka*; the Sultan's violence is converted into a manifestation of divine might. In the context of Morocco as a whole, the Sultan 'eats' the rebel tribes, which leads to his consecration and a gift of life for the entire community. In the local context, only the conjunction of two separate actions, the killing ('eating') of one's adversary in the exchanges of violence and the sacrifice of an animal victim in the peace ritual, gives rise to analogous consequences.

*

Thus far, in the case both of the local tribal groups and of the entire Moroccan community, we have considered the role of *baraka* in specific social contexts, where it orders the unfolding of exchanges among the living and between the living and the Divinity. But this 'divine blessing', unlike honour, is not simply a value which founds the identity of a particular society. Originating in the universal God of Islam, *baraka* permits the *shorfa* to transcend the social categories, limits and prohibitions which it legitimates for the rest of the community of believers.

Indeed, *baraka* manifests itself on another level, beyond the specificity of Moroccan society and beyond exchange, in the mystic brotherhoods founded by *shorfa* ascetics. We cannot analyse here in detail the place of these brotherhoods in the Islamic world, but a few of their principal characteristics may be touched on. The adepts of a brotherhood are admitted simply as believers, not as members of a particular tribe or of the Moroccan community. Entry is the result of individual choice and does not necessarily imply giving up normal activities in the day-to-day world. The mystic *sherif* is the source of a *baraka* which leads each adept from a state of submission to the prohibitions of Islam, which separate Creator from creature, to a union with God in which the believer 'is annihilated (*fana*) in order to abide (*baqa*) in Him'. We detect here the presence of an extramundane individualism which, although not involving a renunciation of worldly life as in India, transcends the confines of Morocco and bears the stamp of the universal value inherent in *baraka*.

In conclusion, this divine force in its holiness encompasses both, at the highest level, the mystic's extramundane individualism and, on a lower one, the Moroccan community as such. Though exchanges of violence were our starting-point, we now glimpse an ideological structure in which transcendence, the recognition of a unique Divinity, is the only absolute, and in which Moroccan society has only relative value. This conception of society and the universe is strikingly different from those found in the two Melanesian societies or at Tanebar-Evav.

Chapter 3

Exchanges, Wholes, Comparison

Exchanges

Our analysis of the exchanges practised by these four very different societies incites us now to attempt a comparison which, as we have already indicated, must treat each society in its entirety, not specific traits detached from the whole which alone gives them meaning. The goal of this comparison is not to develop a model common to the four, nor to formulate a new theory of exchanges. Nonetheless, simply to avow the relativity of cultures would render futile any comparative effort and, with it, the anthropological project itself.

Throughout, our method has required taking into account the entirety of a society's exchanges in order to discover its ideas–values, that is, the dominant facts of and for each society. The propositions which have emerged reveal, in each case, the configuration of a specific 'whole'. Each society thus seems to bear a particular way of being the entire universe. It is precisely in this regard that societies may be compared: in their efforts to administer a universal which is theirs alone. Without an understanding of each society's whole, the observed facts, among them exchanges, would form a vast collection which could only be ordered by imposing the principles implicit in modern ideology.

The subordinated place of subjects

Indeed, had we reduced the problem of exchanges to a simple question of strategies developed by *partners* to satisfy or maximise their respective interests, how could we explain these same partners' submission to weighty, even exorbitant, constraints? If a society's exchanges are not to be reduced to a sum of individual aims, an understanding must be achieved of what there is in them which transcends and encompasses the partners. The latter may, at a sub-ordinated level, pursue personal ends, which are, however, con-stantly recaptured and nullified by the unending repetition of exchanges. Further, are not the partners themselves, be they indi-viduals or corporate groups, constituted by all the different rela-tions which traverse them and cause them to act?

In Melanesia, among the Orokaiva and the 'Are'are, each per-son is considered to be composed of the fundamental elements of the universe – 'image', 'social person' and 'inside', or 'image', 'breath' and 'body'. These are themselves ordered in a hierarchy, in which 'image' expresses the supreme force of the spirits or of the ancestors. By assuring the circulation of the fundamental ele-ments, including their return from beyond death, each society perpetuates itself.

At Tanebar-Evav, a 'house' is not a corporate group founded on unilineal descent but rather a cluster of relations which bind the *yan ur* to their *mang oho* and to 'the god – the dead'. In the inter-play of prestations, the contents – life, the blood contributed by the *mang oho* – 'feed' the containers – 'bodies', houses, sailing-boats – whose tightness in foul weather and impermeability to human misconduct are unceasingly maintained owing to the *yan ur*'s prestations.

In the Rif, not the segmentary units, but rather the 'forbidden domains' constituted by land and women, are the loci where the value of honour encounters the superior value of *baraka*.

Finally, in all four societies, we are led to recognise an impor-tant fact, which is nonetheless surprising for our 'modern' con-sciousness. 'Big men's' 'greatness' in Melanesia, the elders' authority at Tanebar-Evav, and 'great men's' renown in the Riffian cycle of honour, are all entirely at the service of and in subjection to the superior ritual tasks which assure the rebirth and perpetu-ation of these societies and reinvigorate their highest values.

The relational value of objects

Our analysis also reveals that a study of these four societies can-not satisfactorily be limited to a discussion of the movement of a single kind of *object*, be it women or certain categories of goods. While we attempt to explain below the exceptional reach and in-fluence of the model of 'generalised exchange' founded on the rule

of asymmetric marriage, at Tanebar-Evav exchanges are not restricted to the transfer of women. They embrace all the society's
different relations, and their study alone permits the discovery of
the specific whole which the society venerates from generation to
generation.

The Iqar'iyen, for whom women constitute a forbidden domain,
assign no value whatsoever to the exchange of women, but attribute great importance to exchanges of violence, in particular to
conspicuous spending and murder, associated with certain monetary prestations.

The two Melanesian societies place greater stress on exchanges
of taros, pigs and, among the 'Are'are, of shell-money, than on the
exchange of women. A special value is attributed to these *objects*
whose circulation is held indispensable to the smooth working of
the universe, that is, to the reaffirmation of the fundamental unity
of the living with the spirits or the ancestors.

If a particular category of objects is isolated from the whole
which characterises each society and hierarchically orders its exchanges, reality would be arbitrarily oversimplified. The 'same'
objects are attributed different qualities in the exchanges of these
four societies and, within each society, from one exchange to the
next. Their identity cannot be reduced to what we would consider
their materiality, but is fashioned in the course of the exchanges
themselves. Thus, for the Orokaiva, a pig does not become a 'true
reason' until it is raised onto the ceremonial platform at a *pondo*,
just as 'Are'are money, unvaryingly composed of strands of shell-
beads, has different ritual significance at a funeral depending on
whether it ascends onto or descends from the platform constructed
for the feast. At Tanebar-Evav, pigs, rice and millet have different
ritual import in accordance with the sorts of exchanges in which
they appear, as is also the case for metal jewellery and the society's
various other kinds of money. Finally, in Morocco, coins bearing
the Sultan's image play very distinct roles in, say, marriage
prestations or the payment of blood money. The repetitive process of constitution of the same objects and of their different virtues
generally renders futile any attempt at quantitative calculation with
a view to measuring empirical reciprocity, particularly when, as
in Melanesia, the identity of the partners itself is defined by the
exchanges, and since, in all four societies, the actors are subject to
something which transcends them but for which they nonetheless
bear the responsibility.

Exchanges and values

Nor can these societies adequately be described in terms of their social morphology alone. Such a static vision would artificially freeze all movement and award an illusory permanence to the substance of groups or corporate groups. Our resolution to start from a study of exchanges was taken expressly to avoid forcing the movements characterising each of these societies into a morphological straitjacket. The approach adopted has led us to restrict substantially the application of certain classical models. The segmentary system in the Rif, for example, appears much more open than in previous accounts, and reveals itself subject to profound modifications both when honour is at stake and when *baraka* intervenes. At Tanebar-Evav, the houses are seen to be, not fixed units of strict unilineal composition, but rather relays in a complex network of relations between two all-embracing conceptions of the same society. Finally, in the two Melanesian cases, nothing strictly morphological permits us to understand the repetitive permanence of their ritual cycles. To grasp the movement of the whole in these four societies, it was essential to perceive that, in each, the exchanges create a permanent, hierarchically structured sociological locus.

From a methodological point of view, the study of these societies' exchanges incites us to detach ourselves from the strict opposition which modern societies draw between subjects and objects of exchanges and, more generally, between subject and object. Indeed, this distinction substantifies morphological features, which are then organised into rigid, unalterable models. It leads finally to magnifying the subject, become the only indivisible unit, sole seat of consciousness, while society is reduced to a simple collection of the individuals composing it. In anthropological literature, this distinction reappears in the opposition drawn between individual and group. Indeed, the quality of subject, accorded for a time to discrete groups, soon migrated from them to take refuge in the individual, with the result that groups themselves seem to have become the objects of individual subjects. This evolution may be traced from Rivers, who sought to fix once and for all the organisation of groups, to Fortes, who attributed a sort of legal consciousness to them as the foundation of their integration. With Gluckman, groups, while remaining the locus of identity, became in addition the locus where conflicts between individuals are expressed and resolved. The culmination of this process has been reached with Frederik Barth, who inverts the relationship between group and individual in favour of the latter, placing the individual at the hub of multiple strategies while relegating groups to the position of mere objects or means of transactions. The inherent limits we perceive in transactionalism have made it clear to us that a study of individual motivations is neither sociology, given the lack of a clear distinction between subject and group in non-modern societies, nor economics, since the value attached to objects in such societies is not founded upon individual choice.

When the four societies studied here are approached from the angle of their exchanges, the characteristics of these exchanges themselves oblige us to recognise the fluctuating nature of the distinction between subject and object. In the Rif, in exchanges of violence, persons are alternately subject or object, while the segmentary groups appear not as objects but as subjects whose relative position in the segmentary structure evolves in the course of the exchanges. At Tanebar-Evav, houses only come into being and perpetuate themselves as a result of all the different exchanges. In Melanesia, subjects are composed of a transitory union of the same elements which, separated from each other, are found in various objects on which they confer status in accordance with a system of values. Numerous examples illustrate how certain objects are vested with active, changing functions, to such a degree that they are not only imbued with humanity (like taros and pigs, body ornaments and the different sorts of money), but are sometimes attributed supreme value and the power of life and death.

In the four examples proposed, the exchanges permit us to understand the totality of each society's relations and, in doing so, render subjects and objects commensurable. Indeed, subjects and objects intertwine ceaselessly in a tissue of relations which make of exchanges the permanent locus where these societies reaffirm, again and again, their highest values. Relations with the spirits or the ancestors in Melanesia, the values of *haratut* and *lór* in the Moluccas, and the values of honour and *baraka* in the Rif are thus constantly renewed by the exchanges.

Exchanging women or transforming the dead?

The preceding considerations lead us to raise certain questions

about the model of 'generalised exchange' elaborated by Claude
Lévi-Strauss in his theory of kinship.

As this theory asserts, it is conceptually possible, on the basis
of *marriage rules*, to construct paradigms of different patterns of
exchanges of women. On one condition, however. Marriage as a system of exchange must be reduced to the transfer of an object – the
woman – between two masculine subjects (whether or not the
category 'subject' is expanded to include discrete groups), thereby
opening up one of the most important registers of communication
among men. The communication established, if indeed it results
from an integration of the opposition between ego and alter
through reciprocity, makes of marriage a bio-sociological phenomenon in the context of the universal relation between nature and
culture. And even if one wished to assign reciprocity a meaning
as divorced as possible from the empirical sphere, the attempt
would necessarily fail here, given the use made by the theory of
the difference between the sexes as the basis for the distinction
between subject and object. The stage is set, with the male agents
assembled in accordance with one of the possible sets of rules for
the universal exchange of the super-objects, women. If reciprocity
is taken as a universal norm, all relations of this sort are forced, to
a greater or lesser degree, into a mould which sharply separates
the partners to and the objects of an exchange. Finally, if the exchange of women is considered the 'archetype of exchange', a sort
of phylogenesis seems to be postulated, without its being clear
precisely how all the other kinds of exchanges are linked to the
archetype. In the course of this essay, we have seen how many
difficulties are raised by this kind of restriction on the relations
taken into account. Above all, one risks becoming ensnared in the
fundamental concepts of modern ideology. Our attempts to parry
this danger have made us acutely aware of the limitations, and of
the particular orientation of the terms employed to describe relations, from which structuralist analysis suffers.

The rule of matrilateral asymmetric marriage (i.e. marriage with
the mother's brother's daughter) implies the transgenerational repetition of marriages in series, and thus possesses the remarkable
quality of accounting for all of a society's marriages, and even for
the entirety of a given society, understood as the ensemble of relations existing among its groups. But at Tanebar-Evav, exchanges
of women, which may be interpreted as conforming to the model
of generalised reciprocity, are less important in the constitution of

houses than the cycle of life and death ruled over by 'the god–the dead', the *duad-nit*. Furthermore, if the marriage system, associated with the value *haratut*, is indeed subordinated to relations of a higher order between *lór* and *haratut*, it must be allowed that the exchange of women, implied by the rule of asymmetric marriage and constructed on the basis of the distinction between subjects and objects, while integrating the entire society, is simply one specific morphological realisation of an encompassing 'cosmomorphic' circulation in which the distinction between subject and object proves to be quite relative.

This encompassing circulation reveals less a formal arrangement of corporate groups than a pre-existing configuration of values which orders all the society's relations, its various exchanges, and its specific construction of the world. In contrast with Lévi-Strauss' theory, which postulates reciprocity as a universal norm regulating the relations between nature and culture through the exchange of women, our approach is less ambitious, in that we attempt to take into account all of a given society's exchanges before endeavouring to establish their underlying logic. Our aim is not, as one might think, to criticise on an empirical plane the theory of reciprocity as the norm, but rather to propose that the values which order the whole of a society, and not certain of its sub-units, are the appropriate object of comparative anthropological research.

The Hierarchy of Values

The relation with the whole

The use we have made of the word 'value' obliges us, if confusion is to be avoided, to specify the sense in which we employ it. The term 'value' may refer to a subject's intrinsic merit, but also to an object's measurability in relation to other objects which move in exchanges. The two meanings of the word have, however, had divergent histories. 'Value' in the former sense has seen its use sharply restricted, and is now applied only to particular individuals considered in themselves. In the latter sense, on the contrary, it has come to be employed with regard to all exchanges to characterise by comparison all the objects in motion. In economics, exchange value established in the framework of the market is posited, while in current anthropology women have conserved special

value in exchanges. However, as we have noted, in both the economic and anthropological acceptations of the word, an object is
attributed 'value' not because of its materiality but as a consequence of its circulation in a system. Once this point is established,
the limitations of this sort of approach become clear. In the former
case, all objects are considered commensurable in exchanges, and
social reality is flattened onto one plane, called economic, where
subjects are omnipotent and the idea of use value loses all meaning. In the latter, a single object of exchange, women, is isolated,
without knowing precisely how to connect to exchanges of women
all the other objects which with great regularity pass from hand to
hand. In either event, one arbitrarily impoverishes the 'total social
fact' which, in Mauss' view, cannot be understood by starting from
predetermined categories of subject and object. To grasp the entire exchange system of each of these four societies, it is not a question of constructing them on the basis of pre-established concepts,
but of bringing to light the values at work in each totality.

We have seen how mistaken it would be to reduce honour in
the Rif to a particular mode of individual affirmation, when it may
be understood only in the context of the complete system of exchanges. Similarly, the coins of the 'blood money' cannot be considered simply to possess exchange value in the modern sense,
since they incorporate a reference to the Sultan and, therefore, to
the fundamental relation between honour and *baraka*, that is, to a
circulation at a higher level.

Nor is 'Are'are money endowed with exchange value alone.
Rather, the ancestors and their dreadful might are vested for ever
in the strands of shell-beads.

The various sorts of money which circulate at Tanebar-Evav as
well have a ritual weight which manifests the importance of the
fundamental relation between the values of *haratut* and *lór*.

Finally, the Orokaiva of New Guinea only offer pigs on condition that the pact between men and the spirits is renewed at each
initiation and the space of life thus kept open.

One might be tempted to attribute to these objects of a special
sort the quality of 'meta-objects'. To do so, however, would aggra-
vate the difficulties already mentioned by insinuating between
subject and object a new category whose delimitation would increase the rigidity of the distinction between them. We have indeed
seen that certain objects change status in accordance with the ritual
work in which they are implicated. Since value hierarchies are

composed of several different levels, objects take on different relational weight in accordance with the level considered and cannot be attributed a fixed position. Recourse to a class of 'meta-objects', draped in a sort of mysterious abstraction, would only uselessly displace the sharp boundary between subject and object when what is essential is to blur it.

The distinct relational weight of objects on different value levels renders illusory the choice between a theory treating money as a neutral object, simply reflecting the movement of exchanges, and one conferring on money a value of its own, capable of exercising considerable influence on exchanges. If our analysis of 'Are'are society teaches us something about money in general, it is that, as an entity, it plays both of these apparently contradictory roles at once, in reference to a whole whose expression, in this case, is the ancestors. Money cannot exist in the absence of a transcendent order which bestows on it its quality of materialisation of the whole.

From this standpoint, we may well turn the problem on its head and ask, not whether 'Are'are money conforms to one of the possible definitions of modern money, but rather whether it does not reveal unsuspected properties in the latter. Indeed, it seems to us that 'Are'are money and modern money are both, primarily, *money*. It is not so much that the two moneys are of a different nature. Rather, what is distinct is everything that surrounds them. The profound changes which have intervened in our society's values since the beginnings of Christianity are responsible for apparent variations in the role of money, which nonetheless has never ceased to be in direct relation with the whole.

In this regard, 'Are'are money is perfectly adapted to all its society's exchanges, since it upholds and confirms the relative lack of differentiation between subject and object and all the resulting fluctuations in the status of persons and things, while assuring a perfect and very ancient stability in the rates of exchange. Our money, on the contrary, seems less adequate for modern exchanges, since as *money* it negates two of the bases of modernity – the strict separation between subject and object, and the absolute character of the individual subject. Correlatively, wide, uncontrollable oscillations in the rates of exchange become the rule. In other words, the function of money only varies insofar as the ultimate values of societies are radically different.

This digression on the relation between money and value hierarchies clarifies how dependent the concepts of both use and exchange value are on modern individualism and its claim to universality. Use value is necessarily determined in reference to human needs, and thus cannot serve as the foundation for a social theory of value. Exchange value, for its part, presumes a reasonably perfect market, and is supposed to be the resultant of individual wills, tastes and desires. Beyond the market and its institutions, exchange value more generally erects individual wills into a system. The adoption of economic premisses of this sort has doubtless often reduced sociology to confusing a society with a collection of individuals.

In contrast, we employ the word value in its sociological meaning, which incorporates a reference to the totality of the society in Mauss' sense. In every society, certain *ideas–values* perpetuate themselves beyond the life or death of particular individuals, imposing themselves in all the various sorts of social relations. Even conflicts only serve to reinforce them, often in strange disguises, as is clear from the persistence of the opposition individual–collective in our modern subjection to individualistic values. Only through these ideas–values is it possible to accede to an overall comprehension of a society. With regard to each of the four societies considered here, our concern was not simply to describe how its various elements fit together but, above all, to analyse the relation of these elements to the whole. That this relation is a system of values, and not a strictly mental classification, supposes, as Louis Dumont has demonstrated (1986, and really in all his work since 1966), the existence of a *hierarchy of values* composed of different levels of reality or experience. As we indicate below, a comparison of different societies can only fruitfully be undertaken if the hierarchy of each society and its levels of experience are recognised.

Values and the hierarchy of levels

We should note, first of all, that our refusal to posit a priori a separation between subject and object has aided us significantly in bringing to light the fundamental values of these four societies. It becomes possible to 'comprehend' a society when, by beginning from a consideration of its values, we surmount the opposition between subject and object, recognising its relative character instead of treating it as an absolute, with the result that subjects and objects become commensurable throughout social reality: their ontological status is seen not to depend upon this distinction. This is quite clear in Melanesia, for example, where beings and things are defined in terms of the three elements that make up the universe. These elements are endowed with increasing value the more closely related they are to the whole, which among the 'Are'are is also represented by one of them.

Hierarchy is understood here in the sense given it by Louis Dumont, as 'the order resulting from the consideration of value' (1986: 279). This order is characterised by the *encompassment of the contrary* on the highest ideological level, and on lower levels manifests itself as the 'integration of each subwhole as a unit in the next higher one' (Dumont 1986: 250 n. 23). It thus takes the form of a hierarchy of different levels of experience, themselves always inscribed in the overall ideology of the society. The highest level is distinguished by its capacity to define the overall order of the society, while the lower level or levels, although they incorporate exactly the same values, do so in a different hierarchical arrangement and have, consequently, a reduced scope in relation to the whole. The values of a given society can only be understood by identifying these different levels and determining their respective positions in the hierarchy.

A comparison between totalities is certainly never completely absent from anthropological monographs, since every analyst, in seeking to describe the society he has studied, inevitably compares it implicitly to his own. In so doing, he juxtaposes a holistic society, endowed with a hierarchy of levels, and his individualistic society, which is not. In addition to this sort of comparison, the present essay, which treats four holistic societies hierarchically structured in levels, must also confront another totally different and extremely difficult problem. How may four societies of this sort be compared *among themselves*? Or, in other terms, what precisely should such a comparison deal with? Louis Dumont responds: 'Looking at their systems of ideas and values, we can take the different types of society as representing so many different choices among all possible choices. But such a view is not enough to set comparison on a firm foundation and give it a modicum of form. To do that we must take into account the relative importance, in every society or culture, of the levels in experience and in thought that society acknowledges; in other words, we must consider values more systematically than has usually been done in the past . . . [T]he *hierarchy* present in a culture is essential for comparison' (1986: 7).

The living and the dead

But before considering the arrangement of the elements and subwholes of each of these four societies, we should first insist on what the consideration of their wholes reveals at the highest level. All four indeed share the fundamental characteristic that exchanges among the living may only be understood in the framework of relations between the living, on the one hand, and the dead, the spirits or the divinity, on the other. The contrast is striking with our modern society, which situates its exchanges exclusively in the here-and-now by attributing value only to their economic aspect to the detriment of their social component. Modern ideology teaches us to separate the living from the dead. The latter are cast into the realm of belief and animist illusion, and we pay heed only to the former, apprehended consequently from the angle of their corporeal and material activity alone. Indeed, for our modern ideology there is a sharp boundary, defined both legally and medically, between life and death – a living subject becomes a dead object, a corpse. The world of the living is then subdivided by other boundaries into numerous separate individuals (or corporate groups), defined by their corporeity or their real and personal assets.

In holistic societies, these two sorts of boundaries are not insuperable barriers, but rather loci of relation and exchange, that is, of the transformations essential to the perpetuation of being. The fundamental fact is that relations between the living and the dead are not an interaction between two distinct units or entities; they are the primordial manifestation of the encompassing order of each society and, implicitly, of the universe.

The overall order of the Orokaiva is founded upon the relations between men and spirits, that is, between two forms of being, 'social person' *hamo* and 'image' *ahihi*. Among the 'Are'are, relations between men and ancestors evidence a common involvement in the highest ritual task – sustaining the circulation, essential to both, of the universe's three constituent elements. At Tanebar-Evav, the intermarriage relationship links two entities, one composed exclusively of living persons, the other of both the living and 'the god–

the dead' (the *duad-nit*).

The difference between modern ideology and holistic ideology does not repose simply on their respective disregard for or heedfulness to the dead. It consists, above all, in the fact that, while the former accords a central position to the individual and cannot transform the dead, the latter assigns the corresponding position to an association of living and dead in which the living subject, far from representing an absolute value, is completely dependent on an encompassing order that is at the same time social and natural.

Modes of encompassing the contrary

These holistic societies thus have in common their conception of a whole embracing both the living and the dead. Our comparison, to be complete, must however also bring to light the differences in the ways that their various hierarchies of levels are organised. Both in the Rif and at Tanebar-Evav, the different levels of value are characterised by a transformation of the relationship between two discrete values. In the case of the Iqar'iyen, our analysis demonstrated the existence of two levels, one where honour holds sway and *baraka* is latent, notably in exchanges of violence, and another where *baraka* manifests its superiority to honour by rendering fertile the two forbidden domains, women and land. The passage from one level to the other is characterised by an inversion of the relation between these two values, when, for example, a murderer brings a sacrificial sheep to his victim's family, or enters his enemy's house and takes hold of his millstone, suckles at his wife's breast or takes refuge in her skirts.

At Tanebar-Evav, the marriage rituals are at the interface of two levels of value. Exchanges of women and relations between houses, situated at the level *haratut*, are there subordinated to the overall order represented by the whole *lór-haratut*. The inversions noted in the rituals, as well as the 'incompleteness' of certain offerings, manifest the change of level, and make reference to the completeness of the society, conceived of as a sailing-boat. The millet ritual illustrates in a slightly different manner how the rebirth of *haratut* is entirely subject to *lór*, on which it depends for fecundation and protection.

In the two Melanesian societies, where the value representing the whole is entirely contained in the fundamental relationship between spirits and men among the Orokaiva, and between the ancestors and the living among the 'Are'are, our analysis revealed levels of value characterised by an inversion of the relation between the two poles of this fundamental relationship itself.

Thus, in the case of the Orokaiva, at the highest level, that of exchanges with the spirits, spirits prevail completely over men, as is particularly clear in the first stage of the initiation ritual. The essential result of the initiation is, as we know, the complete separation of men and pigs, which opens the way to *pondo* exchanges among men, social subjects and givers of whole pigs. On the *pondo* level, an inversion of the relation with the spirits can be detected, with men now prevailing over spirits. This inversion evidences a change of level, from exchanges with the spirits to exchanges among men. On the *pondo* level, men as social subjects are superior in value to individual subjects moved simply by their 'inside' *jo*. On the contrary, on the *hande* level of exchange, where only pieces of previously slaughtered pigs circulate, individual subjects with their *jo* prevail over men as social subjects. This inversion indicates the change from the *pondo* to the *hande* level.

Similarly, among the 'Are'are, the relation of the living with the ancestors in the cycle of socio-cosmic ritual work on the three fundamental elements manifests the ancestors' superiority, at this level, over the living. Funeral ceremonies are, however, vested with more value than marriage ceremonies, since the former construct ancestors while the latter only prepare the synthesis of human beings. At the level of 'big men's' and 'killers'' feasts, the relation is inverted, with the living now prevailing over the ancestors. In the relation between 'peace-masters' and 'killers', however, the former are superior in value to the latter, since they are portrayed like ancestor-images, and since they offer the money of the 'nine', which, by putting a halt to a series of murders, re-establishes the law of the ancestors and gives new impulse to the ritual work of exchanges on the higher level.

A few additional words may be in order concerning the hierarchy of levels of these two Melanesian societies. Indeed, in the passage from one level to another, in addition to an inversion, these hierarchies manifest certain specific processes which depend on the particular form of each's ritual cycle, but which are nonetheless subject to comparison. Among the Orokaiva, these processes may be called *conjunction–division* and *substitution*, among the 'Are'are, *summation* and *fusion*.

To open the *pondo* level of exchanges, the Orokaiva must first obtain the spirits' agreement to the disjunction of men and pigs. The transformation of the relation with the spirits and the corresponding change of level are corollaries of this *substitution* of pigs for men. Only thereafter need men no longer fear being confused with pigs, which they may thus use as the material of their *pondo* exchanges. Funeral ceremonies, through the combined ritual action of the widow, who makes the mourning vest, and her brother, who provides a pig, make of the deceased a spirit. In this way, the superiority of spirits over men is reaffirmed at the end of the funeral *pondo* as a result of the *conjunction – division* of a pig *hamo* and a vest *ahihi*.

Among the 'Are'are, the socio-cosmic ritual cycle is punctuated by funerals and marriages. Its crucial moments are signalled by two essential monetary summations, one at the conclusion of funerals, the other at the beginning of marriages. The former marks the *fusion* into money of the deceased's three elements (body, breath and image) which the funeral had first separated, and his accession to the quality of an ancestor ('image'), while the latter heralds the resolution of money into the same three fundamental elements on the birth of children. In this ritual cycle, summations and fusions are thus the moments when the passage is made from one level and ontological status to another – at funerals, from the unity of the living person to his separation into the three constituent elements (then all reunited in money), while marriages perform the work in the opposite sense. The same sort of analysis can be made of the summations at the inferior level, affecting only the living, at 'big men's' and 'killers'' feasts.

Orokaiva *conjunction–division* and 'Are'are *fusion* are in some regards analogous processes, but the differences between them reflect important dissimilarities in the superior values of the two societies. Indeed, Orokaiva spirits, the images *ahihi*, differ fundamentally from 'Are'are ancestors, the images *nunu*, since the former are always separate from the 'social person' *hamo* and the 'inside' *jo*, the two attributes of the living person, while, for the 'Are'are, the living result from a fusion of 'body' and 'breath' with 'image'. The different forms assumed by the superior ritual cycles of these two societies are perfectly coherent with the variations in the hierarchical structuring of their fundamental elements. Thus, for example, the use of 'Are'are money is in strict relation with the fusion of the three elements in the living person and with their commensurability in money. On the other hand, the Orokaiva, who only count to two, always rearrange the same two elements, *humo* and *ahihi*. Their ritual work brings about a passage either from *ahihi* to *hamo* or from *hamo* to *ahihi*. Depending on the ritual, pigs are associated with either one or the other of these two elements. In most *pondo*, their separation from *ahihi* creates *hamo*, men differentiated from pigs and spirits, while at funerals, their fusion with *hamo* creates *ahihi*, spirits differentiated from pigs and men.

The following diagrams recapitulate the principal ritual cycles of these two societies.

This schematisation of the two ritual cycles, while omitting a great deal of data, nonetheless has the virtue of revealing very clearly the differences in structure of these two hierarchies of values. The Orokaiva ritual cycle evidences a hierarchical configuration of the type right hand – left hand, in reference to the whole represented by the human body (Dumont 1986: 228–30, 248–9) where spirits and men 'do not have the same relationship to the whole' of Orokaiva society. Indeed, one should 'not separate *fact* (the assumed symmetry) and *value* (the added asymmetry)' (ibid. : 228–30). This value, added to the symmetry, is visible in the position in our diagram of the 'true reason' with its specific property of convertibility. In this system, the 'true reason' stands implicitly for the whole of the society, and evidences the differentiation 'at the same time both in value and in nature' between spirits and men.

The 'Are'are ritual cycle manifests a different form of hierarchy of values in which, what is more, one of the parts, here the ancestors and ancestor-money, represents the whole. The properties of ancestor-money make it much more than the simple sum of the parts or than their temporary union in the living. Fact and value both say separately the same thing, and together – their association is indeed always the foundation of hierarchy – designate the universally convertible ancestor-money as both part and totality.

Orokaiva: cycle composed of two elements and three states

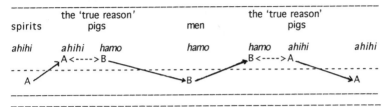

From which it emerges that A and B play symmetrical roles, and that A ∩ B (or B ∩ A) is more powerful than A or B, since the latter always and only give A ∩ B (or B ∩ A), while A ∩ B, on the contrary, can give either A or B.

'Are'are: cycle composed of three elements and five states

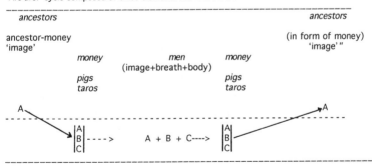

From which it emerges that B and C are interchangeable, while A has a privileged role since it encompasses A + B + C, and at the same time it alone may exist alone.

Toward a comparison of holistic societies

Cosmomorphy

If we return now to a consideration of all four societies, it is note-
worthy that two among them have specific words for their values
– *lór* and *haratut* at Tanebar-Evav, honour and *baraka* in the Rif. The
other two, on the contrary, have no terms for them, which indicates
not that the values do not exist but rather that the societies in question do not formulate them abstractly. In the Rif and at Tanebar-
Evav, we perceive the values as both abstract and concrete. They
reveal how these societies think and speak about themselves. That
words exist to express their values is coherent with the opening
which both of them, each in its own way, manifest toward the
outside world. A society which 'speaks' its values implicitly accepts a universe wider than itself. Further, and leaving aside for
the moment their differences, in both societies the value linked to
the outside is encompassing. The Orokaiva and the 'Are'are, on
the contrary, consider their societies as co-extensive with the universe, have no words for their values, and do not formulate them
abstractly. For this reason, they may appropriately be called
'cosmomorphic', on condition that we understand that this term
itself presupposes a distinction between society and universe,
which modern societies make but holistic societies generally do not.
With the word 'cosmomorphic', we consciously impose, for the
purposes of comparison, a 'modern' point of view on 'non-modern' societies.

For both Melanesian societies, furthermore, beings and things
share the same nature and are limitlessly interconvertible. The
constituents of the person are also those of the universe. The
Iqar'iyen, on the contrary, conceive of their society as a particularity of the universe and revere a Divinity into Whom subjects and
objects are not convertible. This society thus posits a sort of transcendent Subject not exhausted by relations between the living and
the dead. Finally, Tanebar-Evav society, while also recognising
the existence of an outside, only assigns it value as a particular
dimension of the society itself and its own encompassing order.
This characteristic leads us also to consider Tanebar-Evav as
'cosmomorphic'.

If the comparison is extended a bit further, we perceive that in
the Rif and at Tanebar-Evav, the configuration of values is not the
same, although in both cases it is founded on a relation between

two terms. In the Rif, the values, while expressing the social whole, may also be incarnated in specific individual subjects – the Iqar'iyen speak of 'men of honour' and 'men of *baraka*'. Honour, however, does not find its limits in individual manifestations and serves essentially as the foundation of a particular tribal order, while *baraka*, which gives meaning both to the local and the overall Moroccan order, also incorporates a reference to the universal value of Islam. At Tanebar-Evav, the values are two related manners of defining the society itself. Indissolubly bound to one another in the formation of the whole, neither can even be conceived of without the other.

The individual subject and the encompassing social order
What place does the individual subject occupy in the societies we are comparing? In the Rif, *baraka* implicitly refers to a unique transcendent God whose human representative is the *sherif* and, in particular, the mystic *sherif*. Hence, at both poles of value one finds an individual subject, either the 'great man' with his worldly power, or the mystic *sherif*, human representative of a transcendent individual, the Divinity.

At Tanebar-Evav, on the contrary, the values leave no room whatsoever for the individual subject, who can never be the agent bearing the values *lór* and *haratut*. He is left only a residual place, outside the society's value system.

In the Orokaiva and 'Are'are value systems, on the contrary, the individual subject has a recognised though subordinated place. In the former, individual prestations *hande* constitute the lowest level of relations, where there is no repetition and only the subject's *jo*, his socially indeterminable 'inside', expresses itself. In the latter, the 'killer' estranges himself by his conduct both from the society as a whole and from the ancestors, the ultimate value.

Nonetheless, in these two societies the individual subject, although occupying a subordinated position in the value hierarchy, is an integral part of the encompassing social order. For the Orokaiva, every *pondo* exchange is made up of numerous *hande* exchanges, while among the 'Are'are, murder victims have a part in the constitution of a 'big man's' 'image' at his feast. A place is thus left in the encompassing ideology for a sort of unfinished individual subject who, unlike our modern 'individual', is neither complete unto himself nor absolute.

On the basis of these contrasts, we can return to our comparison, and pose the question of the relative weight of these societies' exchanges in their respective wholes. In the Rif, the exchanges are always punctuated by interventions from outside their own domain – the actions of the *shorfa* mediators and of the Sultan – which on each occasion give them a new impulse. At Tanebar-Evav, each time flotsam washes ashore or a person commits a misdeed, *lór* intervenes in *haratut*, breaking into the repetitive ritual cycle and imposing itself in the exchange system. In these two societies, although the exchanges have a fundamental role, they do not themselves exhaust the social order. Among the Orokaiva and the 'Are'are, on the contrary, the ritual cycle imposes a rhythm which nothing can alter, certainly not the individual subject, whose actions always confirm his total encompassment. In the two Melanesian cases, an analysis of the exchanges reveals the whole of each society's ideology.

*

In conclusion, we stress that in developing our comparison we have been obliged to adopt simultaneously two different points of view. To compare these societies as wholes, we have had to found our analysis on a recognition of the place occupied by the observer. From the perspective of the modern observer, the societies presented here all have similar ideologies (facts–values), characterised by a hierarchical organisation in levels of value. The highest level defines the whole and encompasses as well parts which, at an inferior level, are in opposition to it. However, the viewpoint adopted by modern individualistic ideology in seeking to understand holism necessarily blurs the differences among different holistic societies, since it fails to take sufficient account of variations in the way in which the whole of each society is ordered.

A comparison of holistic societies among themselves requires the consideration of these differences as well, to clarify in each case which elements or relations play a preponderant role in the structuring of the whole. Thus, for example, every change of level is simultaneously an *inversion* of the relation between two values and a *division* of a whole of a higher order into subordinated parts, but such changes assume different forms from society to society. In the Rif and at Tanebar-Evav, the *inversion* is apparent in the reversal of the relative hierarchical positions of the terms of certain oppositions expressed in actions, while the division of the whole into parts is so well concealed that only the perspective afforded by a comparative approach enables the observer to detect it. In the two Melanesian societies, on the contrary, the progressive *division* of the whole appears clearly, and is sometimes even theatrically staged in rituals in which some entity – a pig or a sum of money – is physically fragmented into smaller parts, while the inversion of the relation between the values always remains in the shadows.

These contrasts between different hierarchies of values, based on the relative importance assigned to inversion or division, are not perfectly sharp however, since a stress on one of the two processes does not exclude the other, and the extension of each also varies from one hierarchy of values to another. Thus in the Rif, the domain of *baraka* is divided into smaller and smaller parts – the universal community of the faithful, the Moroccan sultanate and, finally, tribal society. From this last level on, however, the inversion of the relation between honour and *baraka* intervenes and precludes a further division of *baraka*. All subsequent divisions, in segmentary groups and in power for example, occur in the domain of honour. Only the passage from one value to the other assumes the form of an inversion, in which the process of division is not pertinent. In the Melanesian societies, on the contrary, the interconvertibility of beings and things renders possible the division of value into smaller and smaller parts, without its ever being necessary to change the value of reference. This difference is no doubt connected with the continuity in Melanesian society between the dead and the living, and the discontinuity in the Rif between the One God and the Riffians' particular society.

In this regard, Tanebar-Evav society occupies an intermediate position, since a ceaselessly reaffirmed continuity between the living, the dead, the spirits and the god coexists with an opposition between two values, two constantly intermingled socio-cosmic references, *lór* and *haratut*. Only the inversion of the hierarchical relation between these two values evidences a change of level.

Finally, our discussion of values leads us inevitably to raise the question of what each of these four hierarchical value systems 'leaves over'. We have attempted to bring out, at each level of value, what is encompassing and what is encompassed. But the latter is never simple to define, since, albeit encompassed, it is never totally integrated. A part always remains which the dominant values do not succeed in assimilating fully, what we call a 'residue'.

Our modern ideology by positing the individual as the supreme value – unique, indivisible and absolute – relegates society itself to this residue (Dumont 1980: 234), and converts a hierarchy of values into something 'shameful'. Among the Iqar'iyen, it seems to us, the value *baraka*, founded on an absolute subject, the God of Islam, encompasses specific Riffian society and the value of honour. The residue which escapes from this encompassing order manifests itself in the 'great men's' pursuit of power. At the other extreme is the individual mystic, whose otherworldly, non-residual perspective places him in closest proximity to the ultimate value. In the 'great men's' dramatic quest for power appears a sort of inverted image of the transcendent omnipotence of God, whom the mystic saint strives to attain for himself and his disciples.

In the cosmomorphic societies, the situation is radically different. Neither the Orokaiva nor the 'Are'are recognise a distinction between world and society. The whole formed by each of these Melanesian societies explicitly encompasses the fully social subject, the giver of a *pondo* or of money for an ancestor's 'image', that is, for the Orokaiva, man constituted of *hamo* or, for the 'Are'are, of an association of 'body', 'breath' and 'image'. At the lowest level, which can encompass nothing and is thus inherently residual, there remains only *the tiny part of man* which is socially indeterminable – his personal initiative, his 'inside' *jo*, or his passions, his 'liver', the part which, paradoxically, for moderns, is the very basis of the subject's identity in its relation to the object. In this descent toward lesser value, one can go no further. From this point of view, Tanebar-Evav society is also 'cosmomorphic', since the continuum which links the living, the dead, the spirits and the god encompasses as well the fully social subject, which in this case is the 'house'; the residual element is constituted by the individual subject.

These three 'cosmomorphic' societies thus reduce to an absolute minimum the residue, which is, furthermore, immediately integrated as soon as it manifests itself. In Melanesia, however brilliant a 'big man's' success, and the more so the more brilliant it is, he is nonetheless completely subject to the order of values, whose most constant servant he is and remains. In the Rif, on the contrary, a 'great man' takes as his inaccessible model the *sherif* of the *baraka*, opening up for himself a field of activity which possesses its own logic, but at the same time remains residual with regard to the society's values.

Bibliography

BARRAUD, C.
1979   *Tanebar-Evav, une société de maisons tournée vers le large*,
                Cambridge University Press, Cambridge – Maison des
                Sciences de l'Homme, Paris
1985   'The Sailing-Boat: Circulation and Values in the Kei Is-
                lands, Indonesia', in *Contexts and Levels: Anthropological
                Essays on Hierarchy*, JASO Occasional Papers No.4 (eds.
                R.H. Barnes, Daniel de Coppet, and R.J. Parkin), pp.
                117–30, The Anthropological Society, Oxford

BARTH, F.
1959   'Segmentary Oppositions and the Theory of Games', *Jour-
                nal of the Royal Anthropological Institute*, 89, pt 1
1966   *Models of Social Organization*, Royal Anthropological Insti-
                tute, Occasional Papers 23, The Institute, London

CASAJUS, D.
1984   'L'énigme de la troisième personne', in *Différences, valeurs,
                hiérarchie. Textes offerts à Louis Dumont* (ed. J.C. Galey), pp.
                65–78, EHESS, Paris

COPPET, D. de
1968   'Pour une étude des échanges cérémoniels en Mélanésie',
                L'Homme, VIII (4), 45–7
1970   '1, 4, 8; 9, 7. La monnaie, présence des morts et mesure du
                temps', *L'Homme*, X (1), 17–39
1976   'Jardins de vie, jardins de mort en Mélanésie', *Traverses*,
                5–6, 166–77
1977   'Des porcs et des hommes', *Traverses*, 8, 60–70
1981   'The Life-Giving Death', in *Mortality and Immortality: The
                Anthropology and Archaeology of Death* (eds. S. Humphrey
                and H. King), pp. 175–204, Academic Press, New York
1985   '... Land owns People', in *Contexts and Levels: Anthropologi-
                cal Essays on Hierarchy*, JASO Occasional Papers No.4 (eds.
                R.H.Barnes, Daniel de Coppet, and R.J. Parkin), pp. 78–90,
                The Anthropological Society, Oxford

COPPET, D. de and Zemp, H.
1978   *'Aré 'aré. Un peuple mélanésien et sa musique*, Le Seuil, Paris

DUMONT, L.
1971   *Introduction à deux théories d'anthropologie sociale*, Mouton, Paris-The Hague
1977   *From Mandeville to Marx: The Genesis and Triumph of Economic Ideology*, University of Chicago Press, Chicago (French edn.: *Homo aequalis 1. Genèse et épanouissement de l'idéologie économique*, Gallimard, Paris, 1977)
1980   *Homo Hierarchicus: The Caste System and Its Implications*, University of Chicago Press, Chicago (French edn.: *Homo hierarchicus. Essai sur le système des castes*, Gallimard, Paris, 1966)
1986   *Essays on Individualism: Modern Ideology in Anthropological Perspective*, University of Chicago Press, Chicago (French edn.: *Essais sur l'individualisme. Une perspective anthropologique sur l'idéologie moderne*, Le Seuil, Paris, 1983)

FORTES, M.
1953   'The Structure of Unilineal Descent Groups', *American Anthropologist* 55, 17–45

GLUCKMAN, M.
1970   *Custom and Conflict in Africa*, Blackwell, Oxford

ITEANU, A.
1983a   *La ronde des échanges. De la circulation aux valeurs chez les Orokaiva*, Cambridge University Press, Cambridge – Maison des Sciences de l'Homme, Paris
1983b   'Idéologie patrilinéaire ou idéologie de l'anthropologue?', *L'Homme*, XXIII (2), 37–57
1985   'Levels and Convertibility' in *Contexts and Levels: Anthropological Essays on Hierarchy*, JASO Occasional Papers No.4 (eds. R.H.Barnes, Daniel de Coppet, and R.J. Parkin), pp. 91–102, The Anthropological Society, Oxford
1990   'The Concept of the Person and the Ritual System: an Orokaiva View', *Man*, 25 (1), 399–418

JAMOUS, R.
1981   *Honneur et Baraka, les structures sociales traditionnelles dans le Rif*, Cambridge University Press, Cambridge – Maison des Sciences de l'Homme, Paris

LEENHARDT, M.
1947   *Do Kamo. La personne et le mythe dans le monde mélanésien,*
            Gallimard, Paris

LEFORT, C.
1978   'L'échange et la lutte des hommes', in *Les formes de l'histoire.*
            Essai d'une anthropologie politique, Gallimard, Paris

LÉVI-STRAUSS, C.
1949   *The Elementary Structures of Kinship,* Eyre and Spottiswood,
            London (French edn.: *Les structures élémentaires de la*
            parenté, 2nd edn., [1st edn. 1949]), Mouton, Paris-The
            Hague)
1950   'Introduction à l'oeuvre de Marcel Mauss', in Mauss,
            Marcel, *Sociologie et anthropologie ,* pp. IX–LII, Presses Uni-
            versitaires de France, Paris
1966   *The Savage Mind,* University of Chicago Press, Chicago
            (French edn.: *La pensée sauvage,* Plon, Paris, 1962)
1967   *Structural Anthropology,* New York, Anchor Books (French
            edn.: *Anthropologie Structurale,* Plon, Paris, 1958)

MALINOWSKI, B.
1922   *Argonauts of the Western Pacific,* Routledge and Kegan Paul,
            London
1935   *Coral Gardens and Their Magic,* Allen and Unwin, London

MAUSS, M.
1924   'Essai sur le don', in *Sociologie et anthropologie,* [1950, pp.
            145–279], Presses Universitaires de France, Paris (English
            translation: *The Gift: Forms and Functions of Exchange in Ar-*
            chaic Societies, Norton Library, New York, 1967)
1938   'Une catégorie de l'esprit humain: la notion de personne,
            celle de "moi"', in *Sociologie et anthropologie,* [1950], pp.
            332–62, Presses Universitaires de France, Paris

POLANYI, K.
1957   *The Great Transformation, the Political and Economic Origins*
            of our Time, Beacon Press, Boston (1st edn., 1944)

RIVERS, W.H.R
1914 [1968]   *Kinship and Social Organization,* Athlone, London

TCHERKEZOFF, S.
1987   *Dual Classification Reconsidered: Nyamwezi Sacred Kingship*

and Other Examples, Cambridge University Press, Cambridge – Maison des Sciences de l'Homme, Paris

THURNWALD, R.
1912   *Forschungen auf den Salomo-Inseln und Bismarck-Archipel*, D. Reimer, Berlin

WILLIAMS, R.
1976   *Keywords: A Vocabulary of Culture and Society*, Fontana, Glasgow

WOUDEN, F.A.E. van
1968   *Types of Social Structure in Eastern Indonesia*, Martinus Nijhoff, The Hague (First published in Dutch, Leiden, J. Ginsberg, 1935)

ZEMP, H., *see* COPPET, D. de, 1978

Index